# Ghosts of
## Southeast Michigan

Kristy Robinett

4880 Lower Valley Road, Atglen, Pennsylvania 19310

**Other Schiffer Books on Related Subjects:**
*Michigan's Haunted Nightlife*, 978-0-7643-3320-0, $14.99
*Detroit Ghosts*, 978-0-7643-3179-4, $14.99
*Ghosts of Anchor Bay*, 0-7643-2302-4, $9.95

Schiffer Books are available at special discounts for bulk purchases for sales promotions or premiums. Special editions, including personalized covers, corporate imprints, and excerpts can be created in large quantities for special needs. For more information contact the publisher:

Published by Schiffer Publishing Ltd.
4880 Lower Valley Road
Atglen, PA 19310
Phone: (610) 593-1777; Fax: (610) 593-2002
E-mail: Info@schifferbooks.com

For the largest selection of fine reference books on this and related subjects, please visit our web site at:
**www.schifferbooks.com**

We are always looking for people to write books on new and related subjects. If you have an idea for a book please contact us at the above address.

This book may be purchased from the publisher. Include $5.00 for shipping. Please try your bookstore first. You may write for a free catalog.

In Europe, Schiffer books are distributed by:

Bushwood Books
6 Marksbury Ave.
Kew Gardens
Surrey TW9 4JF England
Phone: 44 (0) 20 8392 8585; Fax: 44 (0) 20 8392 9876
E-mail: info@bushwoodbooks.co.uk
Website: www.bushwoodbooks.co.uk

Designed by Stephanie Daugherty
Type set in MatrixInlineScript/NewBskvll BT/Humanst521 BT/Fleurons
ISBN: 978-0-7643-3408-5
Printed in the United States of America

# Dedication

To my husband, Chuck Robinett, for driving the Mystery Machine and for protecting me from bats, rats, spiders, and ghosts — but not the demons. My hero!

For my children—Micaela, Connor, Cora, and Molly—for their patience during my writing time, eating cold pizza during deadlines, and for not complaining too much on our Friday night cemetery hunts.

A special thanks to my mom, Sally Schiller, for sharing her love of reading. I hope you are enjoying my stories on the Other Side.

# Acknowledgments

T hank you to all of the homeowners who shared their stories and experiences. Without all of you this book would not have happened!

# Contents

# Introduction

Southeast Michigan is not just a Mecca of industry, but also holds a hidden haunted history. *Photo courtesy of www.sxc.hu.*

*T*he word psychic is derived from the Greek word 'psukhe,' meaning soul. It is applied to a person who has developed either a 'sixth sense' or holds an ability that appears to be outside the possibilities determined by natural law. This includes telepathy, all forms of extra sensory perception, and the ability to foretell the future. But for me, the paranormal not only captivated me, it has been a part of my life since I was a small child because...*I really do see dead people*.

I grew up in Southeast Michigan, the cold streets of Detroit to be exact, in a home that was riddled with spirits and even housed a resident demon that would terrorize my friends and, once in awhile, my family. Needless to say, sleepovers were something of a rarity for me. I wrestled with wondering if the home was haunted or if it was, perhaps, me that was haunted and a beacon for lost spirits.

It was difficult dealing with the spirits that came and went in the old Victorian home. Most of my family members were not experiencing what I was and so that made me a target for ridicule and teasing. As I got older, I went on a mission to prove that I wasn't crazy and that I was in fact witnessing paranormal phenomena. I could often be found with my nose buried in books, reading everything and anything regarding different religions, the occult, and the paranormal, attempting to get clues on how I could prove what was considered unseen. In college, I took psychology and sociology classes and did papers attempting to debunk paranormal events using scientific theory, but that just left me feeling empty. What I learned over the years was to challenge everything with healthy skepticism (scientific method); that process has blessed and enriched my life as I abandoned old superstitions that didn't serve me well or prove valid.

Because of all the Doubting Thomas' in my life, I felt the urge to explore and embrace the paranormal in order to help others who were met with confusion, fear, and frustration. You will see that in many of these stories the homeowners are frightened and are in need of a friend who will simply listen without judgment, something, at times, is far more important than evidence of the haunting. Throughout my years as a psychic and a paranormal investigator I have become a counselor to the living and to the dead. It is a tough job because it lends itself to an open job description, much like the filter you see on a job posting that states "Perform other duties as assigned."

Paranormal phenomena are happenings that require a greater depth of understanding or touch us on a deeper level than normal events. They invoke emotion that is difficult to explain unless you are in the midst of the haunting.

And those around Southeast Michigan have their share of hauntings that come in every form, from spirits to demons to even unexplained winged creatures. Residents of this community are proud of their kids, their cars, their sports teams (well, maybe not the Detroit Lions!), their homes, and even their spirits. They may not advertise their haunting from the rooftops, but it isn't unusual to get into a spirited conversation (no pun intended) with the grocery store cashier who will spill her own ghost story. Or the car dealer who has seen over five UFOs. Or the physician who witnessed unexplained lights in the cemetery near his home.

Southeast Michigan is often thought of as a dingy and stale industrial Mecca that lacks character; however, there is much more than what popular opinion suggests. Southeast Michigan also holds some of the most cultural and diverse areas in the United States, along with rolling farmlands and quaint towns. Each area has its own piece of history and the residents are all very proud of it.

Becoming comfortable with my gift has taken an awful long time and still when I speak with someone who doesn't know "what" I am, I begin with, "Now, I am perfectly sane, but....I see ghosts...." I'm no different from you; in fact, I am actually quite normal. Everybody has the ability to "see." Perhaps these stories will help you believe enough to explore the possibilities. Will you open yourself to it?

# 1

# Tracking the Ghosts

G hosts are people without a physical body. They respond as a person would; they have intelligence, emotion, and personality. The biggest misconception is that a ghost is a demon. That is not the case at all. Ghosts can be negative, but that doesn't make them demonic.

There are highly developed spirits and those that are less developed. Just as you may shy away from or not get along with some human beings in this lifetime, you will also avoid contact with those in spirit who do not have the purest light or vibration. We don't change our personality when we pass away, so if a person on this side was a bully or a thug, they will still be a bully after death.

Many think that the spirit world (heaven-hell) is in some far off never-never land that cannot be reached while still in the physical form. This is incorrect. The spirit world is in the same space that we are in, but in a different form. A spirit identifies with people who have similar values, morals, interests, and ambitions. Just as we are under the Natural Law of Attraction — Like Attracts Like — in our lifetime, spirits are also under that same factor.

Spirits can remain dormant for many years and then suddenly be drawn forward due to tension, stress, and/or emotional problems within a family because that is the vibration that is being put out at that time.

# Types of Spirits

## Spirit Guides

Everybody has a Spirit Guide, whether you want one or not. They are typically not someone you know, but instead someone that is "vibrationally" matched to you and someone you would love on this side. Spirit Guides are with us most of the time and give us guidance on everything from finances to our love life. They often show themselves to us, but not quite in a physical sense.

It was March 2009 when I received a phone call from a lovely lady named Rose. She was concerned because of the activity she was having in her home and asked if I would come and take a peek. She lived in Dearborn Heights, so she wasn't far. We set up the appointment for that same afternoon.

Her home was a brick bungalow that sat on a long street filled with houses replicating hers. Rose brought me some tea and we sat in her family room as she began to tell me her experiences. The more I sat there and listened, the more I kept getting the feeling that there was no haunting at all, but that her Guide was trying to get a message to her. I stopped her, mid-sentence, and asked if she had just had a marital change. She nodded her head and told me that she just divorced. I asked if she had just accepted a new job. Again, she nodded her head and said that although it wasn't a new business, it was a promotion and she wasn't sure she should have taken it, but that it was more money. I smiled and again asked her a question.

"Rose, do you feel frightened by the activity?"

"No, in fact, I don't," she said a little startled. "I actually find it peaceful."

"And is it a shadow that you catch out of the corner of your eye?" I asked.

"Yes," she said in a high-pitched excited tone. "How did you know?"

I knew because it was her Guide offering support to her through all of her life changes. Most of the time you won't feel frightened, just a bit unsettled.

Rose had actually gone to the doctor thinking that something was wrong with her eyes. She had gotten the all clear and so was left without answers until we discussed Spirit Guides.

**Past Loved Ones**
Many times after a loved one passes, they will make their presence known to let their living loved ones know that they are okay. You will feel a sense of peace around this also, but more times than not, they will come in dreams in lieu of an apparition.

I had just had surgery and was put in my room. Frightened because my family hadn't yet joined me, I looked to the chair next to my bed and saw my mom who had passed away two years before. She merely smiled at me and disappeared. It was a comfort to know that I was not alone like I was feeling.

**Poltergeist (Noisy Ghost)**
The most common calls that investigation teams receive is due to a prankster spirit or poltergeist. The most common complaints of these ghostly pranksters are:

🖼 Footsteps

🖼 Low or muffled voices

🖼 Whispers

🖼 Objects vanishing

🖼 Objects being moved

🖼 Cabinet doors opening and closing

🖼 Dark shadows on the wall

🖼 Appliances being turned on and off

🖼 Lights turned on or off at will

🖼 Strange odors

🕷️ Pets acting strangely

🕷️ Your name being called

🕷️ Impression someone is watching

🕷️ Footprints appearing

🕷️ Strong negative emotions felt

🕷️ Rotting smells

🕷️ Physical damage such as feeling slapped, pinched, scratched, or punched

🕷️ Knocks or taps on the walls

🕷️ Scratches on furniture or on the walls

🕷️ Animal noises

Many times these types of spirits are misinterpreted as demons. You have to take in account what else is going around before labeling the haunting as demonic.

## Residual

A residual haunting is in effect an imprint caught in time. The ghost appears at the same time each day, doing the same thing each and every time. It plays back the events over and over like a tape that skips. Residual hauntings are not intelligent and you cannot communicate with these types, which also make it an innocent type of haunting and not dangerous at all.

## Intelligent

Intelligent hauntings often show that they are around. They move items, open doors, make noises, and do anything to make it known that they are around. Many times these types of spirits had either a traumatic and/or quick passing or they still have not realized that they have died. They are sometimes referred to as grounded spirits because many believe that they are grounded to the earth to either fulfill something before crossing over or they are too frightened to cross and are in need of help to cross.

### Demonic

It is very difficult to ignore a demonic haunting. Demons are intelligent and very powerful and absolutely nothing to mess with. I have met several people who have wanted to summon a demon and asked what they would then do with it because they didn't have a clue. Don't attempt a demon summoning and don't attempt to remove a demon. It really is very unusual to have this type of haunting. The more television and movies there are, the more people are calling ghosts a 'DEMON,' but realistically they are very uncommon. But if you do believe that you have a demon, contact a reputable group that has a demonologist on staff or call your local church.

## *Gear and Gadgets*

**35mm Camera** — The good old-fashioned kind. This camera is nice because you can examine the negatives.

**Digital Camera** — I love my digital camera because you can get instant results. However, it is still important to download the pictures on your computer and look at it in a larger field of view.

**Video Camera** — Again, it's good for instant gratification of catching evidence.

**Digital Audio Recorder** — This is important to bring if you want to record Electronic Voice Phenomena, often called EVPs.

**Tape Audio Recorder** — Personally, I am not fond of these because the digital recorder gives clearer sound, but some people like the old school way.

**Electromagnetic Field Detector (EMF)** — It detects fluctuations in electromagnetic fields. Be sure to investigate and write down other things that could cause the fluctuations, such as electrical sources.

**Thermal Detectors or Thermometers** — This is my favorite ghost tool. A drastic temperature change can indicate spirit activity.

**Dowsing Rods** — Dowsing Rods make an excellent ghost hunting tool as they can be used to locate a vortex or high EMF energy.

**Pendulums** — Pendulums work similarly to a Dowsing Rod; however, the pendulum is a very personal tool and is tuned specifically for the individual.

**Extra Batteries** — I tend to drain batteries without being in a paranormally charged environment; however, spirit activity is known to drain batteries, so it is important to bring several extra.

**Flashlight** — I prefer a flashlight that has a red lens on it because when reviewing the evidence, you can differentiate between your flashlight and possible evidence.

**Notebook and Pens** — Log, log, log, log...and log some more.

**Watch** — You need this to aid in logging the time of events as they happen. Many times people rely on their cell phones, however, just like camera and flashlight batteries, your cell phone battery may also drain.

**First Aid Kit** — Bumps and bruises do occur every so often.

**Proper Clothing and Footwear** — Chattering teeth is noisy and can disrupt evidence on recorders.

# Haunted Locations

Most people assume that cemeteries are the most haunted location, but honestly, if I were a ghost that would be the last place I would haunt. In all seriousness, though, there are several places to go if seeking some paranormal activity.

**Hospitals and Nursing Homes**

Being an empath I have a difficult time with both because of the amount of resident ghosts that inhibit these locations, but ask any doctor, nurse, or hospital employee and they will have a story or two for you.

**Private Homes**

A huge misconception is that homes have to be old to be haunted. That is not the case at all. As you will later read, just the history of the land can play a factor in the haunting.

**Historical Homes**

I love the historical homes, which hold endless stories, endless spirits, and an atmosphere to die for. No pun, that is.

**Cemeteries**

I actually find peace in cemeteries. When stressed out from work, I used to walk around and admire the artist's work on the tombstones. It is believed that cemeteries have portals or doorways to the dead, which enable spirits to come and go as they please.

If you're looking for a spirit in a cemetery, the most haunted locations are those that have war veterans, unmarked graves, small children, or stones that date back to the 1700s and 1800s.

**Theatres**

There is so much emotion in theatres, from the actors to the patrons. I went to one local theatre near my town and asked if I could do an investigation. The response was that the theatre wasn't haunted, but in the next sentence the manager added that several deaths had taken place there over the last fifty years. Hmm....

### Churches

Like theatres, churches have so much human emotion attached to them. You have marriages, births, and deaths, which are all emotionally fueled; however, good luck getting permission to investigate one.

### Schools and Colleges

With any large facility, you are bound to get drama—and that doesn't mean the class. Schools and colleges are not exempt from murder, suicide, and deaths. Every facility has its own hidden skeletons.

### Hotels

When I was writing a story about the haunted Mackinac Island, I started with the hotels and began questioning their front desk staff. I was always met with the same answer: "Why, we most certainly do not have any ghosts or paranormal activity in our facility." It wasn't until I began to question those behind the scenes that I got the nitty-gritty of what really went on. I have found that maintenance workers and housekeeping are the most apt to openly talk ghosts.

### Battlefields

With so much violence and mass destruction, you are sure to find one or 101 ghosts wandering about.

## Going on a Ghost Hunt

If you're planning on starting your own paranormal investigation team, I ask you to think again. It would be wise for you to seek out an experienced team. Over the last few years, hundreds of ghost investigating teams have popped up throughout the Southeast Michigan area.

It is important to go with your own gut when choosing a team. Not everybody who investigates ghosts will get a television show, so if you are in this for the limelight, you are wasting your time. Investigating isn't all fun and games; in fact, this 'hobby' takes an awful lot of time, can be expensive, and lends itself to being a counselor to not only the living, but also the dead.

If you want to know what happens on a Ghost Hunt, let me give you a sneak peek:

🦉 The team meets at an agreed upon location at the appropriate time.

🦉 A leader is chosen for the investigation. This leader will speak to the homeowner (if a private investigation), go over the hotspots where the most paranormal activity occurs, and find out what the homeowner wants out of the investigation. Do they want to the spirit removed or do they just want scientific data? I have done numerous investigations where they didn't want the spirit removed...just reassurance that they weren't losing their minds.

🦉 Decide who will work which piece of equipment.

🦉 Teams are divided up, depending upon how large the investigation area is.

🦉 Whether you are in a cemetery or a private residence, I believe it is important to do a protection prayer before beginning. It doesn't have to be religious, but something that puts you into a positive frame of mind and raises your vibration. I have met several people who believed that they brought something back with them from an investigation and, when asked, none of them had protected themselves.

🦉 Walk around the location for at least ten to twenty minutes. Log in weather conditions and any areas that may send off a false reading.

🦉 Set up the equipment.

🦉 Start the investigation.

🕷 Rotate. It is important to rotate the team members. Someone may get something in the kids' bedroom while another team member may not.

🕷 Meet at the ending location.

🕷 Say another prayer of release.

🕷 Go home and get rest!

It is important to note that you should not make any conclusions until all of the documentation has been reviewed.

As an empathic, I do my investigations slightly different than a typical investigator. The team will have me walk through the location and document my feelings along with what I see. I won't ask for or be given any history that will bias what I pick up on. Then I typically leave the investigation. Our notes are compared from their scientific documentation to my psychic and empathic readings. A psychic is just another tool in the toolbox and, although there is no hard scientific evidence with the psychic's notes, it often helps the homeowner not to feel as if they are alone with their experiences.

# What NOT to Do on a Ghost Hunt

🕷 **DON'T use Ouija Boards** — Although this is one of the most debatable topics when it comes to the paranormal and everybody seems to have an Ouija Board story, I would advise you NOT to use an Ouija Board. What is happening when you are so-called "playing" with the Board is that you are acting as a channel and summoning any and all types of spirits to come through. The Board then becomes a magnet for low-level spirits—think the thugs of the Other Side. Do you really want a bunch of spirit goons hanging around you?

**DON'T conduct a Séance** — The same as the Ouija Board. Leave the séance up to an expert (Professional Medium). If proper protection isn't taken, you can open a very ugly vortex. I was at a Bed and Breakfast in Ohio when I was asked if I would conduct a séance. I asked the owner for approval and was met with hesitancy. The owner explained that a very inexperienced Medium performed a séance without her approval a year before and opened three vortexes in the Inn, causing her and the workers a whole lot of grief. After reassuring her that not only did I know what I was doing but that I would also help her with the ghostly problems, she offered her blessing. I did the séance with a group of other paranormal investigators and found a negative energy crouched in the corner of the room, watching us. Gently I talked the spirit into going back through the portal and, as I did that, I sealed the link from this world to the Other Side. Nobody wants to have to clean up after your mess on this side or the Other Side — if you don't know what you're doing, don't do it.

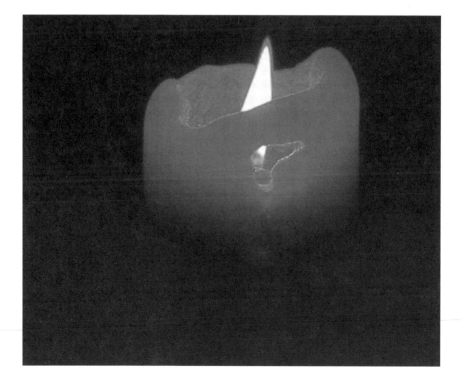

# 2

# Demons in Detroit

I t is plain and simple. I don't much like investigating demonic cases. And yet over the past few years I have received numerous calls from people who claim to have demonic activity. Although I always hesitate, due to my apprehension of dancing toe-to-toe with a demon, I never turn a case away.

My issue with demons stem from my own childhood experiences. I lived in a home not far from this very home that I investigated. My childhood home housed something very evil, very demonic. We felt oppressed, with drastic mood swings. My mom suffered from severe depression, became blind, and had miscellaneous health issues that could never be pegged to a specific disease or reason. The activity in the home flared up when my dad, a deacon for the Lutheran church, began studying the occult for a class that he was teaching. He began to bring home books by Aleister Crowley, a self-proclaimed Satanist, and other books of the dark arts. This, from what I understand now, lent an opening for the evil to slip through. We experienced not only physical issues, but also psychological. In summary, it fed on our fears. One night, my brother returned from working his afternoon shift. He went upstairs to his bedroom and laid down. He kept feeling as if something was stepping on the bed and assumed that it was our cat, Silver. After awhile, when he grew tired of the annoyance, he swatted at what he believed to be the cat and was met only with air. Another night I awoke to a voice coming through my radio warning me to be careful. It ended the ominous warning with a wicked laughter. I ran down the steps, three steps at a time, heart pounding. Demonic activity is nothing to shake a fist to, but it also isn't as common as television and movies make it out to be. In my lifetime (my age I will leave omitted, but it is more than three dozen eggs), besides for my childhood experiences, I have only come into contact with six cases and this is one of them.

The two-story brick home sat in all its glory near Cherry Hill, overlooking Mount Kelly Cemetery in Dearborn, Michigan. The homes around this location date back to the 1920s, each with their own charm. This particular home was no exception.

It was a warm spring day when I visited the owners, Mark and Connie. Pulling up to their home, I admired the cascading old oaks and ash trees. I made a note to see if perhaps the shadows from the trees could be responsible for part of their paranormal claims and played into their fears. However, their story was anything but normal and I discounted the tree shadows immediately upon hearing about their encounters.

Sitting down in the living room, which faced the street, Mark and Connie began to tell me their story.

"We moved here about five years ago. We were so excited to find a house and begin making a family that the last thing on our mind was asking if the house was haunted," said Mark.

"We were more concerned with the plumbing and the roof, you know?" added Connie.

"The problems didn't start immediately. It wasn't until Connie lost her job and then her mom passed away from a long bout of lung cancer that things started to get strange."

"In fact, at first I thought that the noises we were hearing was mom's spirit letting me know that she was okay," Connie explained with clouded eyes. "At least that is what a psychic told me."

Connie went on to explain that her depression grew over her losses. "I didn't know what I wanted to do for a living and I was concerned that we had this new house to pay for. I would stay awake all night worrying."

"I work odd shifts down at the Ford Glass Plant, so I didn't even know she was making a routine of worrying and not sleeping. I am a man, after all," Mark joked.

"During one of my sleepless nights, I decided to come down in the living room and read. I didn't think much of it when the light was on and thought Mark just hadn't turn it off. So I sat down with a magazine and had just opened it when I heard a huge noise. There lying in the fireplace was a dead black bird. It had fallen from the chimney."

"She ran upstairs to our bedroom and woke me up. Honestly I didn't think it was a big deal. I thought she had watched too many movies and read too many scary books. I convinced her to come to bed. I know she tossed and turned because I couldn't sleep either, which is rare. I can sleep through a tornado. Normally."

"The house felt," Connie hesitated and then looked at me, "Unsettled."

I agreed with her. The home did have an anxious feel to it...*almost an angry feel to it.*

Mark and Connie went on to share other oddities that happened.

"It was about a week later after the dead bird incident when I came home from work and saw Connie staring at the wall. She looked like she was in shock. I had to actually shake her," Mark said.

Connie further explained, "I had just gotten home from a job interview and was changing when something pushed me against the bedroom wall. I thought that we had an intruder, but when I spun around, nobody was there. I attributed it then to stress and tried to shake it off, but when I was going down the stairway, I felt something rush past me. As it did, it brushed against me. Whatever it was felt as hot as a stove burner."

"And it left a mark on her right arm."

"All I could do was sit still and pray that nothing happened. Now, I look back and wonder why I didn't leave the house, but it was as if I was paralyzed... I just sat there, waiting until Matt came home from work."

"As soon as she told me what happened, I wanted Connie to immediately leave the house until I could figure out what to do, but she's as stubborn as I am sometimes. She didn't want to retreat, but wanted to get to the bottom of it."

"As each day passed, I started to feel drained. I would wake up in the morning and feel as if I hadn't slept at all. Both of our dreams were so incredibly vivid and none of them pleasant. There was one nightmare that I had where I was walking along the shoreline with this man who I had never seen. He was holding my hand and in the dream I could tell that I was so in love with him. I turned to him to give him a hug and everything turned dark. His face was different; it was red and angry. He reached out for my neck and I knew then that he was going to kill me. I woke up with a start and just shook. It felt so real."

As Connie relayed her story, she began to tremble and Mark reached out to hold her hand. My heart was breaking at how much this was affecting them, but I was pleased to see that it hadn't pulled them apart like many demonic cases do.

"Another incident occurred one night... I crawled into bed, pulled the covers up to my chin, and closed my eyes. I couldn't have been asleep for more than five minutes when I heard a growling sound. In a low, bass tone, I heard a voice that growled my name. The growl continued over and over and sounded as if it was mocking me. With each growl, it felt closer and closer. I began reciting the Lord's Prayer over and over before it went away."

This couple continued to tell me their story as I flipped over my recorder tape.

"Then there are the scents," Mark added. "I will wake up smelling rotting flesh and feel as if someone is standing over me waving rotten meat in front of my face. It then goes away. It feels as if it is taunting us."

"So what would you like me to do?" I asked the couple.

Connie's eyes filled with tears. "We want to start a family and we don't want to move. We love this house. We love the neighborhood and we love this city." The couple looked at one another with decision and Connie firmly stated, "We want to get rid of the demon."

"Now why do you think it is a demon and not just a poltergeist?" I asked.

"Because of the incident with the knives and the crosses," Connie answered.

"I kept thinking that Connie wasn't doing the dishes," Mark laughed.

Connie rolled her eyes.

"Every time I went into the silverware drawer to get a knife, they were gone and they weren't in the dishwasher either. I didn't find them until I went to the garage to get a hammer to hang up a picture — they were all buried, blade up, in the backyard. I freaked."

"So we went out and bought a bunch of crosses to hang up around the house." Connie gestured to the one by the front door. "But we would come home and find the crosses had fallen off the wall. No other pictures, only the crosses. I felt like I was living in the middle of a horror film."

"A hot spot does seem to be the kitchen as it wasn't just the knives that it would take. When we were on to it about the knives, it began to take the forks. Then when we found the forks, it started to just open the cupboard drawers... sometimes when we were right there."

"I can't tell you how many bruises I got from the drawers being opened while I passed by. I kept thinking that I needed to wear football pads when going through my own kitchen."

Connie and Mark had several investigators who had visited and gotten evidence, from EVPs to strange things on camera, but they were at a point where evidence didn't help them. They wanted assurance that they were not nuts, but they also wanted it gone.

Connie began to quietly cry. "I called the Priest, but I was embarrassed. I don't know why, but I kept thinking that he would think we did something wrong. So instead of explaining everything, we merely asked for a house blessing."

Mark took a drink from his soda. "Now we feel terrible for not telling him the whole story."

"As Father blessed the house, he started to get more and more agitated. He later told us it was as if something was dancing around and around him, causing an interruption to his energy. He flat out told us that something evil was in the home and told us to leave," Connie explained.

"And like we said, we don't want to."

"There is good and evil in the world, this side and the other side," I explained, "and I like to believe that good can prevail."

There is definitely a different feel to a demon compared to a poltergeist. For me, the energy feels thick and almost sluggish when there is a demonic presence and this home did indeed have that factor. As I sat there listening to the couple, I could feel us being watched and I indeed felt the taunting that they both explained. I knew that wasn't the night where I could rid the demon. I needed more materials and, since I never proclaimed to be Buffy the Vampire Slayer, I also knew that I needed more information.

I am not afraid of going to the church and asking for help. I'm also not afraid of seeking out other paranormal professionals to aid when they can. I believe in looking for those qualified. I have seen too many inexperienced investigators who believe that investigations are all fun and games and then end up taking on more than they could chew. With this case, I looked to a friend of mine who is a demonologist from another state. He gave me suggestions as to what to do and how to do it and, although I won't explain the exact protocol of what I did to rid the demon, I would like to offer several suggestions if you experience demonic and negative entities *(see "Smudging Instructions" in the Appendix)*.

There was no rhyme or reason to why this family had experienced what they did. Maybe they merely bought the house at the wrong time in their lives, when Connie was going through a lot of life changes, but regardless of the why, I am happy to say that with the help of a priest and a demonologist Connie and Mark are demon free and welcomed a baby girl into their lives last year. Connie does say that she smudges her home on a weekly basis. She says that it is just part of her routine the same as vacuuming is.

# 3

## Ghost in the Mirror

*T*he apartment building was one of many around the Novi, Michigan area. Where farmlands once stood now a variety of buildings loomed, including the apartment building that Cheryl and Joe were leasing.

The ghostly activity began innocently enough with magnets being moved on the refrigerator. Cheryl thought that Joe was moving them just to be funny, but when questioned, he gave her an innocent look. She again didn't think much of it until more and more items were disappearing. Cheryl's car keys disappeared...only to be found in the freezer. Her glasses were continually being moved...only to be found in another room altogether or in odd locations. It began to upset Cheryl because she was very organized; her life demanded it with being a high school teacher at a local school district. Joe would laugh and tease that she was turning into a forgetful professor.

One summer evening, Cheryl sat out on the balcony, enjoying a glass of iced tea. Joe wasn't expected home yet so she was enjoying her time alone by reading a magazine. Cheryl explained to me that she heard a door shut. Startled, she thought at first that her husband had come home, but then realized that she had spoken to him less than five minutes before and he had a twenty-minute drive home from work. There was no way that it could be him. She started to panic, fearing that she had an intruder. She peeked in the window, unsure of what she should do, and saw a shadow run from the kitchen into the hallway. Picking up her cell phone, she immediately called the police and explained the situation. Hanging up, she attempted to call Joe, but his voicemail picked up instead. It only took a few minutes before the police arrived and opened the balcony door for her. They thoroughly searched the apartment, but found absolutely nothing. Joe arrived home just as the police were leaving. Cheryl explained what happened and, instead of being met with concern, Joe was actually upset with Cheryl and informed her that he thought she needed her head checked out.

After hearing that, I grimaced. It wasn't uncommon for a haunting to take over one of the partner's lives while the other was left out in the cold, not experiencing anything at all. I had also seen many couples divorce due to paranormal activity because their tolerance of what was unseen to them and seen to their partner was plain frustrating.

Cheryl did indeed visit her physician to make sure nothing was going on. Because of changes to Joe's work, they had to give up their home and move into an apartment. Joe was afraid that due to the amount of stress, Cheryl was possibly hallucinating. The doctor, however, gave her the all clear and told her to try to get enough sleep. But sleep was a problem.

Every night Cheryl would wake up hearing someone whispering her name. One night, she was startled awake by hearing her name and feeling as if someone was nudging her shoulder. Sitting straight in bed, she looked over at Joe who was sound asleep, snoring. She got out of bed and walked to the bathroom where she stood looking at her reflection in the mirror, wondering why she felt as if she was going crazy. She finally broke down crying. The stress of Joe's job change, the move, and now lack of sleep was just too much for Cheryl to take. As she cried, she felt a presence next to her, but instead of being afraid, she said that the presence felt warm and loving. At that point, she didn't much care what it was—she was going to have a breakdown and not even a ghost was going to stop her. Her tears turned to sobs and the presence drew closer. Glancing in the mirror, she was taken by surprise by what she saw. For a moment's glimpse, she caught the image of a young Native American Indian woman standing next to her. Cheryl blinked and the woman's reflection dissipated.

Cheryl described the lady in great detail to me, right down to a mole that she had on her right cheek. As I listened to her describing her experiences, I continued to feel that Joe was skeptical. I asked him if he had any strange things that had happened to him in the apartment or ever. He met my eyes with a smirk, got up, and walked into their bedroom.

Cheryl shook her head and whispered to me that she was unsure if the marriage was going to continue. She stated that she didn't feel as if Joe was supporting her. She didn't feel believed and she didn't feel as if he was treating her claims as legitimate. It was a lonely place to be.

"I swear that I am not making any of this up," Cheryl pleaded.

I chuckled and told her that she needed to remember who she was talking to — the girl who talked to the dead.

The tension broke and Cheryl smiled. "I just am not sure what to do."

"I wish I could snap my fingers and make spirits appear to those who doubt," I responded. "If I could, I would be a billionaire. But I can't."

We spoke for another half hour or so when I had an idea. I thought that if she had seen the spirit, others also may have and the best person to talk to regarding a haunting when it came to apartments or hotels was usually maintenance. She looked at me skeptically, but at that point she was pretty desperate for answers.

I knocked on the door to the maintenance office and we were met by a man who looked to be in his late 40s. He was mostly bald, with a Detroit Tiger's baseball cap on and a polo shirt with the apartment complex's name embroidered on the left side. I explained what Cheryl had been seeing in the apartment and asked if he had heard of anybody else with experiences. He sure had. He invited us to sit down and shared several stories of murders that had happened near or at that complex (not the same building that Cheryl and Joe resided in) along with history of the land. Cheryl described to him the lady that she saw and he smiled and nodded. He too had seen a woman who matched that description wandering the complex, mostly at night. He said that he ran into her once on a cold winter night. The snow had just started to fall when he noticed a lady walking without a jacket. He stopped and asked her if she needed any help, but she just smiled and continued walking. He said that he started to call her Raven because that was the color of her hair.

There was no concrete evidence that we could give to Joe; however, Cheryl did feel a sense of relief that she hadn't been the only eyewitness to the spirit. Someone believed her.

Cheryl reported to me that she saw Raven several other times—always in the mirror—but her fear had disappeared and she instead felt intrigued...to the point that she joined a local paranormal investigation team and was taking classes on psychic development.

A year later, when their lease was up, the couple moved into a small home nearby. Although they were still downsized due to the economy and job changes, Cheryl reported to me that their marriage was getting stronger with the help of marriage counseling. She also said that her new home felt free and clear of spirits and she was sleeping much better. She added that she hoped that whoever took over her old apartment was functioning better than she had.

# 4

# A Victorian Haunting

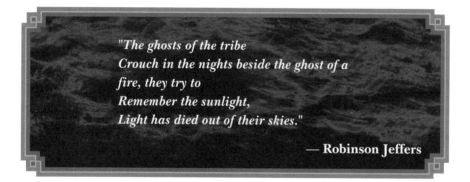

*"The ghosts of the tribe
Crouch in the nights beside the ghost of a
fire, they try to
Remember the sunlight,
Light has died out of their skies."*

— **Robinson Jeffers**

he land currently called Wyandotte has been home to many, but before being populated by Irish, Polish, Italian, and German immigrants, it was home to the Wyandott Indian Tribe.

Wyandotte's history began in the early 1730s when a remnant tribe of the Huron Indians, or the Wendot or Wyandott, settled on the banks of the Detroit River. The tribe was ingenious and set up a city like no other. Chief Walk In the Water was one of the most influential of the Wyandott Indians. He had a strong social common sense and a strong mind and, although the tribe was continually being pushed west by the colonists, the Chief showed that they could co-exist. But the white man was threatened by their intelligence and modern day inventions and, in 1818, forced the Wyandott Indians to sign a treaty with the United States government, relinquishing this land and moving them to Wyandotte County, Kansas, where today remnants of the tribe still reside.

In the 1840s, white settler John Clark, General Macomb, Dr. Delavan, and Major John Biddle founded a "gentlemen farm" on 2,200 acres and called it "The Wyandotte," in honor of the Indians who had farmed on that land. This is the same spot in which the Wyandotte Museum, or the Ford-MacNichol Home, an 1896 restored Queen Anne Victorian home, stands today.

After the 1840s, the history of Wyandotte was mainly shaped by the industries within its boundaries. Drilling produced no fuel, however a large salt bed was discovered — an important

**The Ford-MacNichol Home sits in all her glory.**

**The Wyandott-Huron Indians were an important part of Michigan's history.**

discovery because salt was a key ingredient of soda ash, which was used to make plate glass.

One of the many things I do is organize paranormal events in and around the Michigan area. I love to incorporate history along with a spook factor and, since I had once worked in Wyandotte and knew the area, I had always admired the Ford-MacNichol home. A stately Victorian home, it was built for Laura Ford and presented to her as a wedding gift by her family. The couple, however, didn't stay in it long as they ended up moving to Toledo where Laura's husband opened an industrial plant.

It was early June 2008 when I asked to rent the museum for an annual Halloween event that I host each October. The museum directors informed me that they would have to get approval from the Board, and several week later I received the email authorizing the usage. Plans for a spook-tacular event began to form.

With any event, I began researching the home and the history. Speaking to both the Curators at the museum and librarians at Wyandotte's library, another lovely historical gem called Bacon Library, I received an armful of books and many hours of studying. I liked to hear firsthand accounts, so I began with the employees in the museum, asking if they had noticed any paranormal activity. All laughed at me and said that although the home creaked and they saw shadows once in awhile, they never felt it to be haunted. That was a common answer to most historical locations, so it didn't make me shy away.

As I started advertising the event, I began to receive emails from those who had visited, worked, and lived in the home. Over and over, they shared similar stories, which all validated that yes...*the home was haunted*.

The second family to own the home was the Drennan family. The father was an attorney who had three daughters. After their father passed away, the sisters continued to live in the home.

I was told that the sisters were what you would call the typical ornery old maids. Those who wandered the neighborhood would often see them looking out at the street from the turret windows. It wasn't that their neighbors feared the sisters, but they held respect for them.

A lady came forward who had first-hand knowledge of the home and told me that she had encountered a lot of activity — what could be called *hot spots* — in the Ballroom. She said that it was on the third floor and that I wouldn't be disappointed. Since that was the room that was going to house the lecture, along with the séance, I was intrigued.

Before the event, I did my walk-through, looking over the space. I expected the ballroom to be somewhat elegant, but was met with an unfinished room. Confused if I had received the proper information, I phoned my contact and was told that I was in the correct room. My contact further mentioned that I should pay close attention to the top of the turret window that faced the corner of the street.

Lugging the boxes for the event up three flights of stairs had me exhausted, so I stood on the top of the second floor resting before making another round. As I stood there, breathless, the door to the third floor slammed shut. I jumped and then looked to see if a wind source had caused it, but I couldn't debunk it. It was then that I knew the night would be an interesting one.

**A shadow of an older female, possibly one of the Drennan sisters, is seen in the turret window.**

As each guest arrived, we showed them around the museum, which was decorated in Halloween attire. The front room, decorated to look like an authentic funeral parlor, made for an eerie entrance, but even more macabre was that it was set up exactly as the funerals from that past had been previously in that home. The front room was previously referred to as the parlor and became a place where only social events and funerals took place. Once funeral homes began to open, and we entered the twentieth century, the room was renamed a Living Room or Great Room so that people would feel comfortable in lieu of the sad and mourning implications the room previously had.

Next to the parlor was an office where the museum had set up an authentic embalming table along with instruments. Met with many moans and shudders, it was also one of the most interesting rooms.

A paranormal investigation was done both evenings and each investigation came up with different evidence. The first evening, the basement seemed to hold the thickest energy, as it held many remnants from the past; one such artifact was a piece of the *S.S. Edmund Fitzgerald*. Orbs were plenty in the room next

**At Halloween time, the Museum displays a Victorian funeral.**

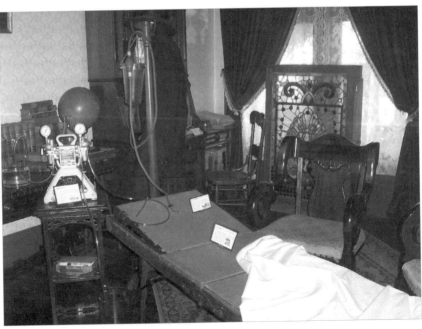

**An embalming table and equipment disturbed many at the conference.**

**The author dressed in period costume for a Halloween event at the grand Victorian home.** *Courtesy of Gayle Buchan.*

The basement of the Ford-MacNichol Home, where many artifacts are kept, gave many conference-goers experiences, including feeling as if they were touched.

Closeup of the orb from the previous picture.

Many orbs were caught throughout the investigation, including the one in the lower right area of this hallway.

to the case that housed it. On the second night, it was the second floor where the Museum office and bedrooms were.

A séance followed each investigation where I attempted to contact the spirits of the home, along with sharing messages from the Other Side for the participants. With four of us on a makeshift stage and an audience filled to capacity, I started by saying a prayer of protection, did a brief meditation for clearing, healing, and centering, and then allowed the spirits to come forward. At one point, the table that we were using began to shake and I felt as if I was about to lose control with a spirit entering my being. I had to stop the séance and ask my husband to sit next to me. This normally helps me to stay focused and, if I can't, he knows how to nudge me out of it. As we listened to the raps and knocks, along with the shaking of the table, we asked yes and no questions. It became apparent that a lady spirit in the house was not happy that we had invaded her beautiful home. Again I had to stop the séance in order to keep conduct. When I call on spirits, I like them to stand in line, much like what you see grade-school students do. That night, the spirits were overly anxious to get their messages through and were creating what felt like chaos. The audience members sat riveted in their seats awaiting their messages.

*Again, I caution you not to conduct a séance; however, attending one with a reputable medium is safe.*

The next night was even busier, in both audience members and activity, with many participants getting instant photographs of what looked like vortexes to orbs (which doesn't always indicate spirit activity, mind you). The séance on the second night was just as busy as the first, with the table shaking. One audience member remarked that she thought the sisters in spirit may actually be enjoying the company and I have to say that I agreed with her. Nothing was negative, but many times cameras failed, batteries were drained, and there were cold and hot spots felt around the home.

In the end, I don't know if I would call the Ford-MacNichol home haunted, but many did have experiences simply by stepping back in time for a few hours to a Victorian Haunting.

# 5

## Mysteriously Haunted

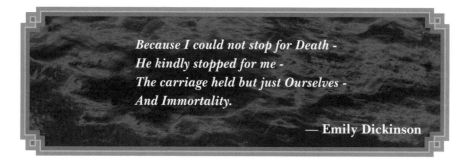

*Because I could not stop for Death -*
*He kindly stopped for me -*
*The carriage held but just Ourselves -*
*And Immortality.*

— Emily Dickinson

## The Carriage House

*T*he Village of Holly is a small town filled with turn-of-the-century charm. Its narrow cobblestone alleys, old-style lamps, and the nationally known Historic Holly Hotel all hold their own stories, spirits, and haunting tales. However, when one unsuspecting single mom purchased a home in the Village, she didn't have a clue that past centuries would intercept with this one.

The small yellow home sat next to the railroad tracks, so close in fact that when the train came by you thought it was coming through the front door. Once a carriage house, the building was originally used to hold buggies for those traveling on the Detroit & Milwaukee Railroad. It also housed something much more. Something secretive...but these days the ghosts have emerged from their hiding places.

Impressed with the school system and the country lifestyle, Sharon and her daughter Amanda moved into the tiny home, which boasted one of the largest trees in Michigan. It didn't take long until they realized that the house was haunted.

Just as everyone would fall asleep, the echoes of singing could be heard; a distant noise, deep under the house, in the crawl space. It didn't happen just once, but every single night. Sharon said that she would inform them that the singing was pretty, but that they all needed their sleep. Unfortunately, the spirits never listened. It didn't take long for those in town to share their own tales to Sharon about the home. It seemed that the small carriage home used to house slaves and had been very instrumental in the Underground Railroad in Michigan. It wasn't documented, but rumored that several slaves had lost their lives waiting for their escape.

The singing wasn't the only thing. The spirits made their presence known continually by turning the radio on each and every night at midnight. They loved to manipulate anything electrical and would turn the lights on (never off). The homeowners would turn them off...only for the lights to turn back on again by themselves.

Sharon and Amanda said that they never felt as if they were in danger from the ghosts and, in fact, they never saw an apparition. Once in awhile they would see flashes of light dance across the walls like orbs, but in front of their eyes. Zero, their cat, would often meow or howl at the air, but Sharon and Amanda grew to co-habitate with the ghosts as if they were their houseguests.

## Doors to Nowhere

The home was often referred to as the 'scary house' in the 1970s. Whenever the kids biked past it, they rode as fast as they could. Today, after forty-plus years, it still stands looking just as it had. What is so bewildering about this home is that it has doors that lead to nowhere.

Although not large or quite as mysterious as the notorious California Mansion named the Winchester House, which has doors and staircases leading to nowhere, this house, a modest two-story home, sits not far from Eloise, the mentally challenged and poor house that is discussed elsewhere in this book. One previous neighbor wondered if there might be a connection.

"Every time I would ride by, I would see an elderly woman with gray hair. I inquired several times as to who the lady was, but was told over and over that nobody living there matched that description," Matt Sheldon, a neighbor who had lived in the area, shared with me. "It was thought haunted by the kids and adults alike. Even today, and I am in my 40s, I still don't like to drive by it," Matt laughed.

The home, still a bit of a mystery, stands much like it did over forty years ago with doors to nowhere.

In the 1960s this house was considered to be the scary house of the neighborhood with doors that lead to nowhere.

# 6

# *Cemeteries Have Spirit*

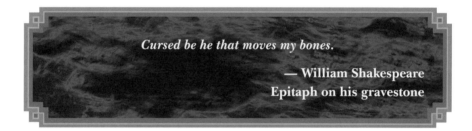

*Cursed be he that moves my bones.*

— William Shakespeare
Epitaph on his gravestone

## *Unexpected Places*

*I* was done with my readings for the day and heading home from the office when I had a strong pull to stop into the cemetery where my grandparents are buried. I tend not to visit loved ones at cemeteries just because I don't need to — I can speak to them anywhere and know they will hear me. I listened to my intuition, however, and dutifully drove in.

With only my memory of where their gravestones were, I found the draping pine tree and parked. Sitting on the ground near their stone, I had an instant flashback of when I was all of eight-years-old and my grandpa had passed away. I saw the funeral, those in attendance, and felt the sadness of everybody — especially of my mom. Tears began to fall and I wondered why I had been drawn to feeling that sadness. A bird chirped above me, nudging me from my sorrow, and it

was then that I saw her. Sitting in a lawn chair with a baby boy was a beautiful woman with long brown hair. She held the boy's hand and stared at the grave. It was obvious that the funeral was recent as cascades of flowers were freshly laid on the dirt mound. I sat for a bit, wondering if my sorrow was more hers than of my own past memory.

Before I could conjure an answer, the little boy quickly crawled down from the chair and toddled over to me, plopping himself down in my lap. I was startled. He looked up at me and smiled a knowing smile. I tasseled his hair, gathered him up, and walked over to mom who was as stunned as I was. She apologized and sat back down with the blonde-haired boy in her lap. Her emotions were static in the air. I asked if she was okay and if she wanted to talk. I won't go into detail, but this young mom, now a widow, poured her heart out to me — a perfect stranger. I listened. I cried. I hugged her. No, I didn't tell her 'who' I was; I wasn't at the cemetery to drum up business. I do, however, firmly believe that my grandpa, who was such a bright light, knew that this young girl needed someone to talk to and knew that I was just the person. I have to say that I don't regret trusting my intuition, and I thank grandpa for sending me to unexpected places.

By using your intuition and opening yourself up to the Other Side, it will lead you in new directions and open new doors. Trusting your intuition is the key that unlocks those very doors, and acting on it allows you to walk through the doorways to new opportunities...it will lead you to unexpected places.

When beginning ghost hunting, cemeteries are a great place to start. In Michigan, it is illegal to be in a cemetery past dusk, so it is very important to either ghost hunt in the daytime or to ask permission from the office for an after-hours investigation.

I happen to love cemeteries. In fact it is one of my favorite places to visit. On any vacation, you will see me yell for my husband to pull the car over so that I can explore, and I admit that I stop at a cemetery at least once a week.

Cemeteries and everything in them have very important value to everyone who has ever known anyone buried there. Every statue, every small symbol, every epitaph has an important meaning to the ones who know what to look for. The way to create the gravestones and their architecture come from different places all around the world, but they all meet in one place. Everything there is to honor the dead and to show the living that life will go on, even if it's after his or her own death. I find cemeteries to be one of the most peaceful and beautiful places on earth. Don't believe me? Stop by a turn-of-the-century cemetery and wander. The tranquility of the environment will most certainly calm you.

There is much debate over whether or not a spirit can follow from a haunted location; however, I have had it happen not only to me, but also my clients. And just read *Aaron's Crossing* by Linda Alice Dewey; in it, she shares her story of bringing a spirit home after visiting a cemetery in Northern Michigan. So whether you believe you can or believe you cannot, it is still best to protect yourself before you enter a cemetery and again letting the spirits know that they are not welcome to come along for a ride when you leave.

With so many favorite cemeteries, I had a difficult time choosing which ones to include, but I do believe you will enjoy each one of these just as I do. But again I ask that if you visit them, please respect the posted laws and those buried there.

## *Thayer Cemetery*

### Northville Township, Michigan

Thayer Cemetery, named after Rufus Thayer who was the original landowner, is located in Northville Township on Napier and Six Mile roads. The cemetery dates back to 1811 and sits next to an abandoned schoolhouse that looks of the same time frame. As you peruse the gravestones, you will also see that it houses many other members of the Thayer

Thayer Cemetery sits at Napier and Six Mile roads and dates back to 1811.

An old schoolhouse sits abandoned next to the cemetery.

One team member, a talented psychic, felt drawn to the schoolhouse, stating that she felt like someone was there watching her.

The cemetery was named after Rufus Thayer, who was the original land owner.

family, as it was, which was typical for that time period, a family cemetery.

I have visited this location several times with my group and always received a feeling of being watched, followed, and even touched. You cannot rely on your clairsentience (scent), however, as the cemetery sits kiddy corner from a dumpsite.

The cemetery is in disarray and it is disheartening to see how it is uncared for by the public, as I have witnessed tire tracks, tombstones knocked over on purpose, and graffiti on the schoolhouse.

## *Yerkes Cemetery*
### Northville Township, Michigan

I had an odd experience with this cemetery. I would drive by it frequently on the way to my 'real' job, however this was one cemetery that I had never stopped at...*until I had a dream.*

It was a Saturday night when a handsome young male spirit visited me. He was dressed in a Civil War uniform and

**After a visit from a ghost soldier, the author stopped at this cemetery to find dead animals atop his grave.**

he informed me that he was buried in Yerkes Cemetery. He told me that I must go to his grave, but wouldn't explain why. That Sunday, after church services, I asked my husband to swing into the cemetery to see if I could find the young man's stone. Thank goodness my husband is so patient and tolerant of my crazy dreams and visions! Camera in hand, it didn't take me long to find his grave and find out what was causing his distress. On the gravestone of this soldier were the remains of dead animals, completely gutted. I called the police department and reported the macabre findings, leaving the soldier to, once again, rest in peace.

## *William Ganong Cemetery*

### Westland, Michigan

The William Ganong Cemetery, located on Henry Ruff Road between Annapolis and Van Born roads in Westland, is noted as one of the most haunted cemeteries in the Michigan area. Many believe this to be the case because of Eloise, a historical and haunted mental hospital that is nearby but now closed, along with an abandoned field where over 7,000 bodies are buried in unmarked graves.

Named after a local farmer William Ganong, he and several of his family members lay at rest in this wooded cemetery. Unfortunately, because of its haunted notoriety, it is a ghost hunter's haven along with those who perform rituals of the more dark magick type.

The William Ganong Cemetery is considered one of the most haunted cemeteries in Michigan. One of the tombstones reads an eerie epitaph:

"Behold ye strangers passing by
As you are now so once was I
As I am now so you must be
Prepare for death and follow me."

This cemetery is often called Butler Cemetery because there are close to twenty Butlers buried here.

Ganong was formed in the 1830s, named after a local farmer William Ganong. There are many haunting stories from a lady who is often seen wandering the streets and causing car accidents. The only experience that I have had in this cemetery is my camera shutting down and photos disappearing. This happened the day that I went out to take the photos for the book. I received one, but that one was not fantastic quality. Is this paranormal? You be the judge.

Nearby the William Ganong Cemetery is a field of unmarked graves named Eloise Cemetery or Potter's Field. These graves lay in a field, marked only with a number.

**This field holds over 7,000 dead in unmarked graves.**

## *Oak Grove Cemetery*

### Dixboro, Michigan

Dixboro, primarily a farming community, is near Ann Arbor, Michigan, and is a one-streetlight type of town. Mere blocks from town sits Oak Grove Cemetery. Sheltered with many trees, this small cemetery dates back to the 1800s, with many of its ancestors in unmarked graves in a field mere blocks away. The intriguing story behind this cemetery is that it is noted as being haunted by Martha Mulholland, who was murdered by her brother-in-law.

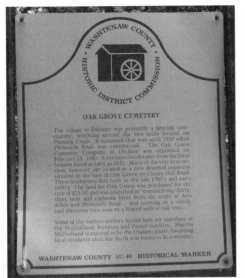

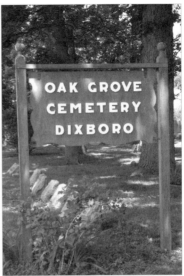

OAK GROVE CEMETERY

The village of Dixboro was primarily a farming community, revolving around the two mills located on Fleming Creek. It remained that way until 1925 when Plymouth Road was constructed. The Oak Grove Cemetery Company of Dixboro was organized on February 24, 1860. It contains headstones from the local farmers dated as early as 1831. Many of the very first settlers, however, are located in a now deserted cemetery situated to the east of Oak Grove on Cherry Hill Road. These headstones date back to the late 1700's and early 1800's. The land for Oak Grove was purchased for the sum of $25.00 and was described as "commencing thirty-three rods and eighteen links from the angle of Ann Arbor and Plymouth Road... and running in a south-east direction nine rods to a blazed yellow oak tree..."

Some of the earliest settlers buried here are members of the Mulholland, Freeman and Parker families. Martha Mulholland is reputed to be the Dixboro ghost, haunting local residents until her death was found to be a murder.

WASHTENAW COUNTY  SU-40  HISTORICAL MARKER

**Dixboro has its tales of murder and ghosts and Oak Grove holds just some of those secrets.**

**Martha Mulholland once haunted Dixboro after being murdered by her brother-in-law.**

## *Oakwood Cemetery*
### Wyandotte, Michigan

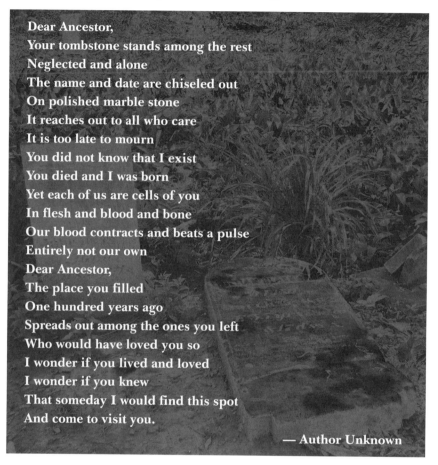

Dear Ancestor,
Your tombstone stands among the rest
Neglected and alone
The name and date are chiseled out
On polished marble stone
It reaches out to all who care
It is too late to mourn
You did not know that I exist
You died and I was born
Yet each of us are cells of you
In flesh and blood and bone
Our blood contracts and beats a pulse
Entirely not our own
Dear Ancestor,
The place you filled
One hundred years ago
Spreads out among the ones you left
Who would have loved you so
I wonder if you lived and loved
I wonder if you knew
That someday I would find this spot
And come to visit you.

— Author Unknown

Oakwood Cemetery is the oldest cemetery in Wyandotte and one of the oldest in the downriver area. Volunteers work tirelessly, caring for and restoring the neglected cemetery that has been in disarray with long grass, weeds, and deep holes ever since the late 1800s when ancestors moved away and stopped caring for the stones.

I advise caution when visiting. Not for the spirit activity, but for the possibility of injury by tripping or falling from the poor conditions. Visit in the daytime and peruse the stones and their history.

**Oakwood Cemetery has some of the most beautiful statues, including this angel.**

This cemetery is difficult to obtain evidence from due to a manufacturing plant that sits next to the cemetery, on the Detroit River. Because of this, you may want to use dowsing rods, pendulums, or psychic abilities in lieu of electronic equipment, which may not prove to be reliable. Many who have investigated this cemetery have had experiences even with the noise. At the far back corner of the cemetery, another team member and I felt someone nudge us on our shoulder. Both of us looked back, only to see nothing there. It is the presence that makes this cemetery worth investigating.

## *Rural Hill Cemetery*

### Northville, Michigan

Rural Hill is one of the most peaceful cemeteries that I have encountered. Tucked in the back of Northville, it has gravestones that date back to the early 1800s. It was here

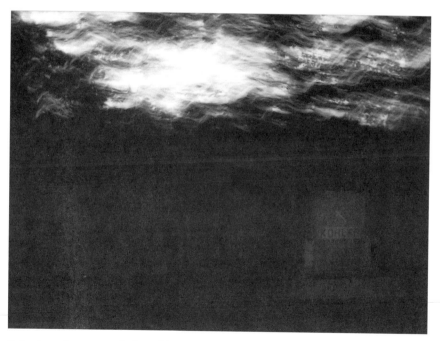

Ectoplasm is commonly found in pictures of Rural Hill.

**When investigating Rural Hill, investigators saw what looked like a fairy sitting on the tombstone and snapped this photo.**

that I received several strange photographs, taken with two different types of camera. Each time I have visited, I have had experiences...none spooky, but instead serene.

## Chubb Cemetery

### Livonia, Michigan

Located on Warren Avenue, west of Hix Road, sits thirty-seven plots that makes up Chubb Cemetery. It's named after Glode and Pamelia Chubb, who owned farmland at that location; Chubb was known in the area for his participation in the Underground Railroad during the 1830s.

Although difficult to retrieve EVPs due to it being a high traffic area, using other instruments — dowsing rods and EMF meters — yields positive results. A serene and happy feeling was here everytime my group visited. It could be that the good Chubb did makes even the spirits content.

## *Kinyon Cemetery*
### Ann Arbor, Michigan

Kinyon Cemetery is located at Ridge and Gyde roads, maintained by the Canton Public Works, Leisure Services, and the Canton Civitan Club. Although it is in pretty good condition, it holds its share of snakes and squirrels that like to throw acorns at visitors. It also holds several spirits...some thought to be on the negative side.

Several broken tombstones lay on the ground and beside the large trees that loom high. Many of the stones date back to the mid-1800s with the most recent burial taking place in 2000.

Kinyon Cemetery is in my book as the most active cemetery that I have ever investigated. With each investigation, everybody on the team has experienced something. We have never been disappointed... *During an investigation on one warm July night, all of the members were pushed in unison. The night was bright with a waning moon and there was no wind. There was no other explanation other than plain paranormal.*

Large orbs are often found in pictures taken at Kinyon Cemetery.

It is said that a doorway to the other side is in this cemetery and that spirits come and go at will.

Orbs and rays of light would follow team members.

The flares of light could be seen without any equipment.

## *Shearer Cemetery*
### Plymouth, Michigan

Shearer Cemetery is an abandoned
cemetery off of North Territorial Road in
Plymouth, Michigan.

Shearer Cemetery is an overgrown and abandoned cemetery that sits north off of North Territorial Road in Plymouth, Michigan. Easily missed, it is a steep climb high upon a hill. Most of the stones have been moved or are crumbled and unreadable.

If you sit quietly on the bench that stands in the middle of the cemetery, you will hear whispers. Some say that it comes from the spirits, but others say there are faerie rings and the

It's a steep climb, but high on a hill sits a magical cemetery.

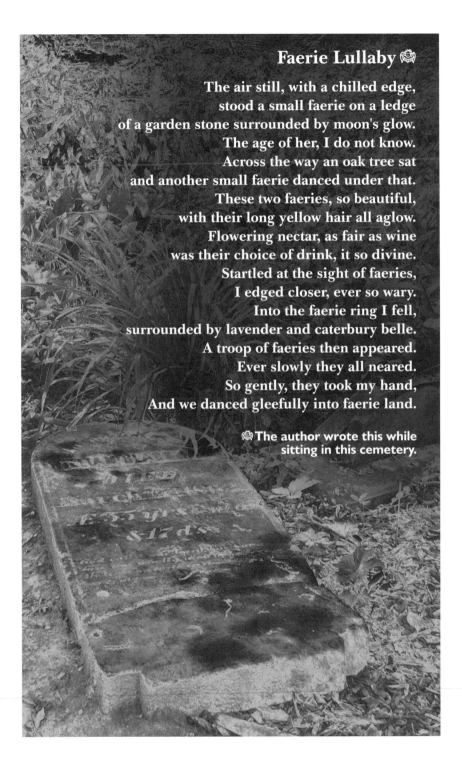

### Faerie Lullaby

The air still, with a chilled edge,
stood a small faerie on a ledge
of a garden stone surrounded by moon's glow.
The age of her, I do not know.
Across the way an oak tree sat
and another small faerie danced under that.
These two faeries, so beautiful,
with their long yellow hair all aglow.
Flowering nectar, as fair as wine
was their choice of drink, it so divine.
Startled at the sight of faeries,
I edged closer, ever so wary.
Into the faerie ring I fell,
surrounded by lavender and caterbury belle.
A troop of faeries then appeared.
Ever slowly they all neared.
So gently, they took my hand,
And we danced gleefully into faerie land.

The author wrote this while sitting in this cemetery.

faeries wander in the lily of the valley, hostas, and other flowers that bloom.

## Newburg Cemetery

### Livonia, Michigan

Paranormal groups flock to Newburgh Cemetery as the energy in these historical grounds is thick. Orbs and vortexes are easy to get and EVPs are often obtained when investigating Newburgh.

**This tree has grown around a tombstone.**

**Newburgh Cemetery originated in 1827.**

# Cemetery Etiquette

1. **Obey the Laws.** Read the posted signs. If it, in fact, says that there is no entrance after dusk, obey that.

2. **Respect.** Respect the deceased. This is their home, so treat it as if you are visiting with a friend. Don't litter, move statues or gravestones, eat or drink (do so outside the cemetery). Have fun, but watch the jokes. You may in fact anger a spirit by being disrespectful with careless jokes.
   You also need to respect the living. If you are ghost hunting while mourners are there, please respect their time. More than likely they don't want you trying to catch an orb of their Uncle Joe.

3. **Be a Team.** Never ghost hunt alone. It isn't that a spirit will injure you, but the living might. Someone on another team had decided to ignore this rule and went out alone. He tripped over a rock and broke his ankle. This brings us to our next rule, another one he hadn't followed....

4. **Communication.** Always bring your cell phone with you. If you're with a group, it's also nice to have walkie-talkies for updates when breaking up into small groups.

5. **Ask.** Ask permission from the spirits to take their photo, videotape, or record. You aren't the paparazzi. If you feel a light feeling — go ahead, an angry feeling — think twice.

6. **Pets.** Don't take your animals on a ghost hunt. It just isn't appropriate. A number of things can happen such as the animal being spooked by a spirit to desecrating the grounds.

7. **Don't smoke.** Not only is it bad for you and others, it contaminates the investigation and photos.

8. **Log weather conditions.** Check the weather report and document everything from the precipitation to the humidity. This will help as you debunk your evidence.

9. **Do a walk-through.** If you are going to the cemetery in the dark, make sure to go through it first in the daytime as to avoid potential hazards.

10. **Hold the cologne.** Many people utilize their sense of smell during investigations as a spirit can manifest with a perfume, smoke, or other type of scent.

11. **Batteries.** Always bring extra batteries. There is a phenomenon called 'Battery Drain,' where it is thought that when spirits manifest, they first drain the batteries of electronic equipment. To be on the safe side, always use fresh batteries at the beginning of each investigation and bring backups with you.

12. **Say NO to drugs and alcohol.** By impairing your judgment, this could endanger yourself and others. Use common sense.

13. **Wear appropriate clothing and footwear.** I once went ghost hunting with a girl who had on stiletto boots. Her heel became stuck in some muck. Refer back to the use of common sense.

14. **Carry your identification.** Even if you have permission to ghost hunt, concerned neighbors may in fact call the police.

15. **Don't whisper.** This may surprise you, but by whispering instead of using an inside type voice, it may damage evidence on your tapes.

16. **Bring backup flashlights.** A light source is important during both daytime and nighttime investigations.

# 7

# Doorbell from the Dead

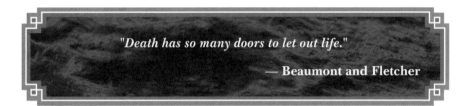

Christine was excited about the move. The divorce had taken a toll on her and her two young children and they were all excited about a fresh start. The new home was only a mile from their previous homestead, but she had purposely done that as not to disturb the kids with school changes. It was just that their old home had been in her ex-husband's family and it was too painful to stay there, not to mention the acre of land that she just didn't have time to cut. The new start would be good and, when Christine found a gem of a three-bedroom ranch in Westland, Michigan that boasted a great price, she signed the paperwork as fast as she could.

The move took place a week before Christmas, and to say that it was a tad overwhelming for Christine to move in the snow, unpack, finish holiday shopping, decorate the home and the Christmas tree, along with all the other stresses that the holidays bring, was an understatement. Christine, though, was what many would describe as an overachiever.

The actual move went fairly smooth. That first night Christine stayed up late, attempting to organize and put everything in its proper place. The house was in remarkable shape with polished hardwood floors, built-in bookcases, a natural wood burning fireplace, and a finished basement with a family room, laundry room, workshop, and bathroom. Although the basement wasn't the typical creepy kind, she still hated it for reasons she couldn't explain. Setting up the kids' toys in the basement, she kept feeling as if someone was standing right behind her and would continually look over her shoulder to see if perhaps the kids had snuck down, but nobody was ever there. She chalked it up to being in a new home.

Christine finally fell asleep around midnight, but woke up at 3 a.m. and pulled the blankets up around her neck. She was freezing and not even the down comforter could keep her warm. Moaning, she got up to see what the problem was. Turning on the hall light, she saw a tall black shadow dance across the living room wall. Figuring it was a reflection from a car's headlights, she shook it off and looked at the thermostat. The dial, which was manual and not electronic, was switched to the off position. Baffled, she wondered if perhaps the kids or her dad had played with the thermostat before bed; she flicked the switch and trotted back to bed.

The alarm rang at 6 a.m. and, with the night's drama, it felt much too soon — and, once again, the home was frigid as she crawled out from underneath her mountain of blankets and awoke the kids. Even though they were off from school for Christmas break, she still had to go to work. She looked at the thermostat once more and sure enough the switch was at the off position. Again, Christine turned the heat on and began her daily ritual of making hot tea, taking a shower, and preparing the kids' breakfast. As they sat down for their waffles, she asked her 6- and 8-year-olds if they had touched the thermostat and they both looked at her curiously, not even knowing what a thermostat was…that in itself was telling.

Once at work, she called her dad and, explaining the strange incident with the heat, asked him if he would go over and check out the house. He promised that he would stop over and offered an explanation of a bad thermostat. It was less than an hour when she received a call back from her dad stating that the heat was in fact off when he got over there and that she better call a furnace guy as soon as possible. The temperatures were dipping well into the low teens and the last thing she needed was frozen pipes. She moaned and prayed that she hadn't just bought a lemon of a house. Christine knew just the person to call. Her old neighbor owned a heating and cooling company and she immediately phoned and made arrangements for Mike to meet her at the house as soon as she got off work.

Being the dependable guy that Mike was, he was already in her driveway waiting for her when Christine pulled up. She unlocked the door and offered a summary of the situation. Mike told her that he would change the thermostat and check on everything else, but he added that he had never heard of such a thing. Christine offered to make him some coffee, of which he gratefully accepted, and so, after showing him to the furnace room in the basement, she went up to the kitchen to turn on the pot.

"Christine?" Mike called.

Christine met him at the stairway, just off the kitchen.

"Were you just downstairs?" Mike asked.

"Uh, no, I have been here the whole time making coffee," Christine answered. "Why?"

"Well, someone pushed me when I was leaning over checking out the pilot light and, as much as I figured that you weren't playing a trick on me, I had to ask."

Christine looked at him sideways.

"I don't see anything wrong with the furnace, Christine. I think you have a ghost," Mike joked.

Mike was the sensible type. His boyish charm made the girls swoon, but he was a faithful husband and a wonderful dad to his only daughter...and he was completely sane.

Christine didn't want to accept that explanation. Honestly, she was a businesswoman who had never even had an encounter with the unexplained. She laughed it off. Mike changed some parts just in case and went on his way. That same night, with the kids away at their dad's house, Christine slipped into bed around 9 p.m., plain exhausted from the previous night's ordeal. She fell asleep watching television, but woke up to a loud noise. Startled, she grabbed her cell phone and checked the time — 3 a.m. Her doorbell rang once...and then again...and then continually over and over. She peeked out the bedroom window and saw nothing. Her window looked out to the side of the home, so with her heart pounding, she went into her son's room and looked out his window, which gave full access to the front door, but was met by absolutely nothing. Yet the doorbell continued to ring. Opening her cell phone, she dialed 911 and asked for a patrol car to come by. Hanging up her phone, the doorbell immediately stopped ringing.

Christine sat on her couch, huddled in her fluffy white robe, and waited for the police to arrive. In just a matter of a few minutes, she saw the lights from the patrol car and eagerly met them at the door. They asked what the problem was, and she explained the ringing of the doorbell. The patrolmen smiled at one another and informed her that they were often called out for similar situations and that it was probably the neighborhood ghost. They went on to explain that the neighborhood was rich with Native American history and that many of the Indians were buried in that same neighborhood from battles long ago. Electronic equipment was easy for the spirits to manipulate and gain the attention of innocent homeowners.

In March, three months after moving in, Christine was cleaning up her yard when she stopped one of her neighbors. Sheepishly, she asked if they had ever had problems with ghosts. The neighbor nodded and shared some eerily similar circumstances with her.

Christine's home sat in the neighborhood of Tonquish Sub, named after Chief Tonquish. Not far from her home was the burial site of Chief Tonquish, who had resided on the banks of the Rouge River. In 1819, farmers were searching for food and came upon Chief Tonquish and his sons. There was great resentment between the tribe

**Chief Tonquish and his son.**

**Often times the spirits of Indians can be heard by the river of where it is believed Chief Tonquish was killed.**

and the white man as they were trying little by little to push out the Indians. It was then that they killed Chief Tonquish and his sons and buried them. A plaque marks their burial site, which is located at Joy and Wayne roads, and the suburbs around there are noted as Tonquish Sub, with street names indicative of that time period including Chirrewa, Mohawk, and Bison.

Christine stayed in the home for less than a year. Although the house was beautiful, the spirit activity was very active and she felt drained every morning, haunted by vivid dreams of battles. Her strange electronic malfunctions continued occurring where the lights would flicker on and off, light bulbs would be unscrewed, and the washer would stop working only for nothing to be wrong with it. Christine said her breaking point was when she took a shower. When she got out, she wrapped herself in a towel and went to brush her teeth. When she looked at the bathroom mirror, scrawled in the steam on the mirror was what looked like hieroglyphics. It was just too much stress for a single mom to take. She made sure to move out of Tonquish Sub and informed me that her new home was ghost free and she was coping much better.

# 8

# Demons in Our Dreams

*"Evil enters like a needle and spreads like an oak tree."*

— **Ethiopian Proverb**

When I first began writing this book, I received an email from a family who stated they had a demon in their home in Plymouth, Michigan. I was entranced, as it wasn't everyday that I received a demon call; however, I was also a tad bit suspicious. So, I called and spoke to the daughter, Kendra, who assured me that her mom's house boarded a demon...if not more than one. Since my intuition told me that Kendra sounded sane, I made an appointment to meet her and her mom Maggie the following week.

At that time I was still working my corporate job and just so happened to be on a break when I had called Kendra to obtain more information. Little did I know that my boss was outside of the break room listening in on the conversation. After hanging up my cell phone, he dutifully called me into his office and told me that he didn't know what I was doing, but that it had to stop immediately. I probably looked at him funny, because I was merely getting a story. I have since resigned from that position, but looking back, I am sure that listening to an employee talking to someone on the phone about cleaning the house of demons is quite abnormal, although it is a normal part of my life.

The morning of our meeting, I awoke with laryngitis and felt like death warmed over. My head was clouded and I had absolutely no voice, so I emailed Kendra and explained the situation, apologizing the entire time. We scheduled an appointment for very next week and, once again, I came down with something that prevented me from meeting with them. Again, we rescheduled for another date and time. The night before my interview with them, I had a horrible dream that to this day is as vivid as ever. I was in a black room with just one small light that acted as a spotlight. In walked a creature that looked like a man, but was maroon in color. His eyes were hollow and he growled as he neared me. He didn't speak in words but telepathically — and I heard him tell me that I would suffer greatly if I went to the house. I woke up and was too frightened to go back to sleep and encounter that being. I sprinted from my bedroom and lay down on the couch, pondering what I should do. I finally fell asleep out of exhaustion, but even after waking, I could feel its strength and its power around me. I knew that whatever this was, it was the same thing haunting Kendra and Maggie.

Because I tend to be the stubborn Scorpio, I had already told myself that I wouldn't allow this demon to tell me what I could and couldn't do. Okay, maybe it was called stupid instead of stubborn. So, with my husband in toe as my demon-guard, we made our way just a few miles from my own home into the town of Plymouth, Michigan.

It was a sunny spring evening as we traveled west to Plymouth. We hadn't received any rain in a few days and the temperatures were quite pleasant. Just as we pulled into the homeowner's driveway, we noticed the neighbors gathered around in a commotion. Getting out, we could see a very large tree that had just fallen and the neighbors were discussing the oddity of a healthy tree dropping out of nowhere on a beautiful day. My husband and I looked at one another and knew that the demon was once again trying to prevent me from meeting the family. Once again, though, I had it in my head that no matter what, I was going to go through with the meeting.

The home was a typical 1970s style ranch that sat on the main road. I grinned at the "For Sale" sign in the front yard, knowing that whatever this creature was, that in no way was it going to allow the sale of this house.

I was met at the door by Maggie who offered me a hug and walked us to her dining room. I had my digital recorder. Before turning it on, I said a prayer of protection and then began the interview. Maggie told us that they had lived in the home for approximately ten years and, while they had always had strange activity, it had increased since the passing of her husband. I told her that I wanted to discuss a dream that I had the previous night that kept me from sleeping, as if the dark circles under my eyes weren't an indicator. I gave her the play by play. Maggie's eyes widened as she completed the last part of the dream. She too had been warned that I was not to come.

I sat across from Maggie, with my husband on my right. In back of me was a window that looked out into their backyard. The more we spoke, the more the energy seemed to be disturbed until it felt like we were being played with and it wasn't Duck, Duck, Goose either. I could sense a shadow in back of me, but ignored it as if I was ignoring a four-year-old needling their mom with the "Mommy... Mommy... Mommy... Mooooommmmmy..." In the middle of the interview, my husband stood up and said that he couldn't take it anymore. The *thing* had touched him several times and he was angry because he didn't know how to stop it. Excusing himself, he left to sit in the car. My demon guard was gone.

Sitting in the corner near Maggie sat a statue of a man holding a serving tray. I looked over at the statue several times only to see it wink at me. I thought perhaps it was my lack of sleep that was making me see things when I saw it do it again. I cussed myself out for not bringing a video camera. I asked Maggie if she had noticed the statue doing anything unusual. She laughed and said that her husband had loved that statue. She also said she wouldn't be surprised if it was her husband protecting me since my own had run off.

Maggie and Kendra began sharing stories of the haunting. Maggie asked if I was interested in looking at some photos and she went into her bedroom and grabbed the originals. As I examined the photos, I was a bit taken by one photo in particular of a skeleton leaning over a family member. They had taken the photo in the garage during a party the summer before. I might have written it off to smoke, but with the dark feel of the home and the previous night's dream, I believed it to be true.

Kendra and Maggie asked if I would like a tour of the home and I nodded, grateful to get away from the dizzying energy that surrounded us. Just as we went in the back bedroom, a light bulb blew and I wondered if it was another warning. As we walked around, they continued to share stories of being attacked at night, hearing it call itself Satan, to seeing black orbs move through the kitchen into the living room, and even hearing heavy breathing voices. We went down the basement and I instantly felt nauseous, which made me consider that perhaps it wasn't paranormal and instead a high electromagnetic field, of which prolonged exposure to can cause anything from headaches, fatigue, dizziness, skin rashes, weakness, increased anxiety, and what they call a "fight or flight" response. We continued the tour when I caught sight of a crawl space underneath the garage and inquired the use of it. Neither was sure of the purpose, but said they also always wondered. I ended the interview and asked if I could bring a full-fledged team out...one that had a demonologist on board. They both agreed and said that the church had been in and out several times blessing the home, but that it hadn't helped at all.

I couldn't wait to get out of the house.

That night I dreamt of the crawlspace below Maggie and Kendra's garage. In the dream I saw skeletons buried underneath rising up and haunting the house; creating chaos in their lives. I sent Kendra an email, asking her to check out the history of the house and again asking for permission to bring in a team. The emails were left unanswered for at least another year. Kendra said that they had decided after I left to try and ignore the activity in hopes that it would diminish enough for the home to sell. Unfortunately, it hadn't worked and the activity had only increased.

This case is still open as we figure out the history of the home. Still today, anytime I am scheduled to visit the house, I get sickly and have come to realize that this may not be my case to solve, but another's. This demon may be someone else's battle, but until I find that person, I hold the sword.

# 9

# The Checkered Coat Angel

*If you still believe that angels are those things that wear*
*fluffy white wings and fly, I ask that you re-think that.*

When I was a child, I walked everywhere. My mom was blind, so it was a requirement that if we wanted to go shopping we had to hoof it. Every week, on our way to the grocery store, we would come across this man who looked to be in his 30s, tall, skinny, with warm eyes. He would meet us on one side of the street and help us to the other side. He often would tell me to smile or offer a compliment. One day, we were sitting in Sanders eating an ice cream and the man came in looking agitated. I was probably about seven at the time, but I picked up on his emotion and asked him if he was okay.

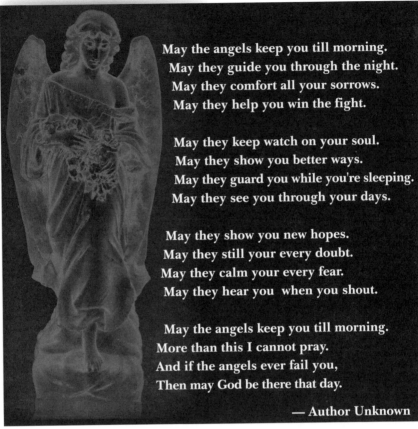

May the angels keep you till morning.
May they guide you through the night.
May they comfort all your sorrows.
May they help you win the fight.

May they keep watch on your soul.
May they show you better ways.
May they guard you while you're sleeping.
May they see you through your days.

May they show you new hopes.
May they still your every doubt.
May they calm your every fear.
May they hear you when you shout.

May the angels keep you till morning.
More than this I cannot pray.
And if the angels ever fail you,
Then may God be there that day.

— Author Unknown

His almond brown eyes lit up at my concern and he nodded and told me that he was supposed to help someone, but that it didn't work out and he was being assigned elsewhere. When he left, he offered me a hug and told me to always remember that I was special. We never saw him again. My mom thought perhaps he had mental issues, but I didn't see it. It was all a mystery. It wasn't until several years later that I realized that he was an angel, perhaps sent to help my mom, and, ironically, I could see that whether as a human or an angel, the frustration of not getting through to someone was similar.

It was a June day when my husband, kids, and I headed to the local pet store in Livonia, Michigan. The location where the store sits is where a racetrack used to be housed several years ago. I noticed an elderly man standing in front of his car with his cart in front of him and I 'knew' he needed help. I nudged my husband and asked him if he would offer him assistance since I, myself, had just had major surgery. The four of us walked over and my husband asked if he could help. The man looked at us as if he was going to cry. He went on to say that he had spinal cancer and probably didn't have long to live. He was okay with that, but he was frustrated that he could no longer use his arm to lift anything and further explained that his pets were important and needed to be fed regardless of his health. Chuck obviously loaded the items in the car and helped him into the driver's seat. The man continued to thank us, but in the end it was all of us that were moved. This man wasn't just 'some' man...he had an energy about him that the only way I can explain was angelic. Now that wasn't the reason why we initially helped him. I didn't sense that until we got closer and only wanted to cry in pure love.

As we watched this man drive off, we all wiped away a tear. I turned around once more, but the car was gone...as if it had vanished in thin air.

Do you believe it is a mere coincidence when that friend calls you out of the blue right when you need a word of encouragement? The Universe (God/Goddess/whoever you believe in) places people in our paths every day of our lives, but we sometimes turn our backs to them. They come in all colors, sizes, ages, and geographics, and rarely wear white fuzzy wings and play the harp. You may not recognize them the instant you meet them, but that is okay — as long as you open yourself up to accepting the help that they are offering. There are truly glimpses of Heaven right here on earth and some of those are called Earth Angels.

I was telling my story to a store attendant who looked at me in awe. She asked me what he looked like; I told her that he was lanky and tall and had a checkered coat on. She said that she had a similar encounter with the same man, but not in her store, but at another in the same plaza. She said it was during a time that she was having a difficult day and was just perusing a shop to keep her mind off of everything when the man came up to her and offered a smile. He told her that she looked very pretty and that he knew things would get better. She said she smiled back, looked away, and then look back towards him and...*he was gone*. So who is this checkered coat angel? After doing some research, it is thought that he had been a regular at the Detroit Race Track. A perpetual smile on his face and love in his heart, he doesn't haunt. Rather, he spreads love.

# 10

## The Lost Kids

*L*aura was fed up. Since moving into their new home, she hadn't slept. The feeling of being watched was so overpowering that she would wake up with a start, absolutely sure that someone was standing on top of her. She didn't even feel safe taking a shower. She said that the feeling bordered on being stalked. Then there was the laundry room in the basement…she would run in and run out as fast as could be. Her husband laughed at her and most of her family thought she was just being overly dramatic, but she knew what she felt and she didn't like it one bit. It wasn't until her large dogs — a black lab and two pit bulls — began to react by barking and staring at absolutely nothing that she decided something had to be done. That was when she contacted me.

It was a warm summer day when I made my way south to Garden City to Laura's three-bedroom ranch. Her husband greeted me at the door, asking if I was the psycho...errr…

psychic. Thankfully, I have a sense of humor and greeted him with a laugh and a sideways look. Immediately, I knew that this investigation would be different. Upon entering the home, I, too, felt as if I was being watched. Instead of doing the customary preliminary interview, I asked if I could tour the home to see what I picked up on. Her husband, John, or more like Mr. Skeptic, charged ahead, showing me the areas that his wife had claimed she felt things. After touring the first floor, I asked to go into the basement — and what I found there was downright frightening.

As I neared the bottom of the steps, I could make out the spirit of a man who was at least 6'5" tall. He wore a tall black hat that was similar to ones you see Abraham Lincoln wearing in pictures, which would be indicative of the mid 1800s. He had shoulder length black hair and dark, menacing eyes. The scariest part was that next to him there were spirit children. He held a little boy's hand in his left hand and a little girl's in his right — both looked about six years of age. Their eyes pleaded at me to help, but they didn't speak. A rush of cold air brushed past our faces and he was gone.

We continued the tour, but the spirits didn't reappear, so we sat down to map out a plan. I told John and Laurie that I was concerned because of the spirit children and that I wanted a night to sleep on it and do some research. John, now becoming a tad bit more of a believer by the second, and Laurie apprehensively agreed.

That night, I dreamt about the spirit children who introduced themselves as Alice and Eli. They told me that the man I saw them with was named Martin and that he had been a child molester in the 1860s and had kept them hostage. Eli explained that the town they lived in had discovered Martin's crime and they were planning on hanging him. Martin caught wind of his execution and contrived a plan that involved kidnapping them and using them as hostages. The plan backfired, however, and Martin ended up killing Alice and Eli and then committing suicide. Before they could cross to the light, Martin grabbed them and has been keeping them hostage in the afterlife ever since. Tears fell down Alice's cheeks. Eli comforted her. My heart ached.

The next morning, I prepared my bag of tools and called Laurie to see if I could go over to their home that evening. I was apprehensive to tell her of my dream because I didn't believe it was a dream at all, but the true story behind the haunting. Anything to do with kids, whether living or dead, pulled at my heartstrings and I knew that I had to help. Armed with bay leaves in my pocket and white sage, sea salt, holy water, and geranium oil in my bag of tricks, I knew that I was ready.

As soon as I entered the home, I could feel the anger. John and Laurie informed me that the previous night had been especially active with doors slamming and the opening and shutting of kitchen cabinets. I could tell that Martin *knew* and hoped he hadn't hurt the kids. As I made my way downstairs, I could see Eli and Alice huddled in the corner, frightened. I gave them a reassuring smile and started my 'attack' on Martin. I knew I had to get him to go first and then help the kids into the light without Martin pulling them away.

I began by smudging the home with the white sage and saying a prayer, asking over and over for the children to be safe and shrouding them in white light. I then began my steps to have Martin leave. I prayed for at least a half an hour as Martin paced up and down the stairway. Utilizing sage, sea salt, and holy water, I called on the angels to remove the spirit from the house so that he could meet his Maker. I wish I could say it worked like you see on television with a flash of light and a peaceful energy, but I can't. Martin didn't cross, but his energy did feel tired, so I instead worked on helping the kids cross. I spoke to them just as I would flesh and blood children and urged them to seek the refuge of the light. Their fears were spoken once more that Martin would grab a hold of them and they would be punished. It would take time.

The following week I returned to the home. Laurie stated that the energy felt clearer, but she could still hear footsteps in the attic and continued to be on edge in the bathroom. As I explored the home, I could not find the spirit children, but I did find Martin. His anger had turned to what felt more like sadness and depression and it was then that I realized that the kids had gotten enough strength and courage and had crossed, leaving Martin alone.

I didn't feel bad for him at all. He had been a bad person on earth and had attempted to be that same horrible person in spirit. He had to cross and meet his judgment. I knew that the spirit wouldn't listen to me, so I once again began my ritual of ridding a spirit and called on an army of angels and all of our guides to cleanse the house. Again, Martin began to pace and feel antsy. It wasn't as if I was hurting him, but I was evicting him from his home and he was afraid. He was afraid of what he would find once he crossed and I didn't blame him. After completing the process, I once again left and asked Laura and John for updates.

It was the very next day that Laura called to let me know that the house felt quiet and that she was grateful. I can't tell you if in fact Martin crossed or if he possibly took residence somewhere else, but Laura and John, the self-proclaimed skeptic, didn't want to take any chances and ended up moving. They felt that the house had bad Mojo and they wanted to start fresh...*without* spirits...and *without* Martin.

# 11

# Horror and Haunts

*L*ivonia, Michigan is a large suburb in northwest Wayne County, just fifteen miles from Downtown Detroit. Known for being a safe city and having wonderful amenities such as community centers, libraries, and police departments, it also houses the unknown.

The young couple was thrilled with their recent engagement and were just as excited about moving into a new home. Both Tracy and Larry had been married before and both had kids, making it a priority that their new house be in a good school district. When their realtor showed them a four-bedroom, tri-level in Livonia, Michigan within their budget, they grabbed it immediately. The schools were just a few blocks away and the neighborhood was full of kids. Making it even more appealing was that their family lived nearby. With wedding plans and a move that combined the two families, looking back they decided that they were either too stressed out or just not paying attention to the paranormal activity that was going on, and chalked the strange occurrences up to mere coincidences. At first it started with innocent things such as shoes being moved, keys disappearing, and candles being blown out. Tracy and Larry would blame the kids, who would claim that they didn't do anything, but kids would be kids and they figured that they were just not fessing up. When the activity in the house became frightening — *and there wasn't an explanation* — that was when I was called on to investigate.

Tracy called me on an October afternoon. The weather in Michigan was still quite warm, an Indian summer, with the temperatures reaching the mid 80s. The pitch of her voice made it clear that she was frightened and she needed help immediately. Since her home was mere blocks from my own residence, I went over in the evening to do an initial interview.

During the interview process, Tracy, Larry, and I sat in the living room to discuss the activity. It was disheartening to see this newlywed couple, who should be worrying more about who was going to do the laundry and what flowers to plant in their new garden, were overwhelmed with what to do about a ghost.

"It started the first night we moved in," Larry shared. "We had only moved a few boxes into the home, but we were so excited about the home that we decided to spend the night."

Tracy continued, "We felt like kids. Sitting on the hardwood floor with a bottle of wine and Dixie cups, we shared a drink in celebration. We were chit-chatting when all of a sudden the bottle broke, spilling the rest of the wine all over the floor."

"What really made us feel unnerved was that it was June and although it was not overly warm out, it wasn't cold either and as we cleaned up the glass and wine, the colder the house got...to the point we were shivering. I thought that the inspector had left all the windows open, but that wasn't the case."

"The scariest thing that happened was when we were sleeping and I thought that one of the kids had gotten up in the middle of the night. I got up to check on them and went down into the basement bedroom where my 15-year-old slept. As I climbed the last stair, I felt as if there was an invisible door there because I couldn't move. I was transfixed to that spot. I could see Greg in his bed, sitting up, and he was crying for *it* to leave him alone."

Tracy looked at me, "You know, when it is your child in danger, you will do anything."

I nodded. I, myself, had four kids and when the spirits start to interfere with children, it made me downright upset.

"I gathered all of my energy and pushed through into his bedroom...only to be felt as if I was being pushed back. I started praying and felt a sense of peace throughout the room. Greg got up from his bed and we hugged, thankful that it was over. But after that the kids were scared to sleep in their own beds and this is where we all sleep," Tracy pointed to the living room where they had a brown sectional couch.

Tracy and Larry shook their head, still in awe. The activity continued from June until the day that I met with the couple. They were so frightened that they moved their kids out and they were staying with their ex-spouses because they felt it would be safer that way.

The homeowners began by giving me a tour of their immaculate home that sat in the Rosedale Gardens suburb between Merriman and Farmington roads and West Chicago and Plymouth roads. It houses bungalows, colonials, and ranches and is known for its tree-lined streets, park, and the many gardens that bloom.

Tracy and Larry's home was a typical Colonial with four bedrooms, all on the top floor, but this home had been remodeled with a gorgeous basement that included a family room and bedroom. Their living room was a good size, with a bay window with stained glass, and their view was that of the quiet tree-lined Livonia neighborhood.

Walking through the home, I felt as if I were being followed and turned around several times to see who was behind me, but nobody was. The energy was thick and felt dangerous...not like a typical haunting...not like a typical ghost. It felt like so much more than that. I asked about a small room the size of a workshop in the basement. Larry stood in front of it, as if protecting the entrance. Puzzled, I told him that I respected every piece of his privacy. He hung his head down and opened the door and turned on the light. The room was a sanctuary for everything horror...from figurines to posters to videos. There wasn't anywhere to move.

"This is Tracy's obsession," Larry explained.

"Fascination, not obsession," Tracy corrected, shyly.

Horror movies and merchandise from the same isn't evil, but the energy of fear that exudes from it can certainly stir up something that already exists, and I explained that while I wasn't going to have Tracy ditch her memorabilia, we were going to have to find a way to shut the portal of energy that was feeding from it.

I went around the home, smudging it with white sage and asking my Guides and Angels to clear the home of all negatives. As I lit the smudge stick, a large breeze kicked in and the flame burned my right hand. I knew that it wasn't going to be easy, but that with several tries we would close the portal so that this young family could enjoy their home and start to live their lives.

As I continued to say the prayers, along with the homeowners, Tracy became more and more agitated. She began to cry and then she started to get angry with me, demanding that I leave at once. Larry took me aside and confessed that Tracy's mood swings have been getting completely out of hand the last few weeks to the point that he was frightened of her. With Larry's assistance, he made an excuse and took Tracy to the local convenience store, leaving me alone in the home. I continued to smudge, realizing that the energy felt clear. It was then that I realized that it was not the home—it was Tracy who was haunted.

When the couple returned, I sat down and explained to them that not only can homes be haunted, land can be haunted and so can people. It was then that Tracy admitted that she had always had unexplained paranormal activity around her, but thought that she was a freak. I counseled her on different tactics that she could use to protect herself. From sea salt baths to visualization, to amulets and crystals that could act as protector so that she didn't have to feel as if she was fighting a battle. I also asked that she go to the doctor's for a check up. Sometimes hormonal issues, depression, or vitamin deficiency can play into unexplained supernatural issues.

It has been over a year and the kids have since moved back into the home and everybody sleeping back in their rooms without any problems. Tracy did in fact decide to sell off her collection and get help for her depression. She told me that she also wears a Black Onyx pendent that she says has helped her to feel more grounded. All of these steps helped to make the home and the family peaceful and clear of negative energy.

# 12

## Earthbound Souls

### Saul

*"Ghosts crowd the young child's fragile eggshell mind."*

— Jim Morrison

*T*eresa was having problems with her little boy. Not that it was unusual for a three-year-old to misbehave; however, he was becoming more and more disruptive and argumentative. She stated that Aaron rarely slept and when he did it was fitful, but she was most concerned because he was speaking to someone...even playing with someone...and yet *nobody* was there. She wondered if perhaps he had Attention Deficit Disorder and was at her wits' end. If it has anything to do with kids, I am immediately on alert. Having seen spirits since I was three, I was curious to investigate the property to see if it truly was Aaron or if they were having a haunting.

I drove to Teresa's home, which was in a remote area of Romulus, surrounded by woods and farmland. Parking my car, I grabbed my purse and immediately felt someone push me back into the car. Taken by surprise, I got up and, before shutting the door, I realized that I had forgotten my cell phone in the center console and leaned over to retrieve it. I again had an eerie feeling... It was as if someone was standing right in back of me.

I walked up the landscaped driveway and was met at the door by Teresa and Aaron. The air in the home was a collection of anxiety and worry intermixed and I immediately felt that perhaps Aaron was an empath.

Empaths are sensitive beings who are quick to pick up on emotions, whether good or bad. Empaths can walk into a room of people who are angry or who just had a disagreement and feel angry or sad and not know why. The biggest challenge for an empath is to decipher if it is their own emotion or someone else's. With the tension in the air, I felt that more was going on with this family than what was being shared.

Aaron immediately came up to me and held his hand out for me to hold. Teresa looked stunned and shared that Aaron was not a warm and fuzzy type and that he never allowed anybody to touch him. I graciously accepted Aaron's hand and, bending down to his level, I started to talk to him.

"Did mommy tell you why I was here?" I asked.

"Yes, she says you see ghosts. I see ghosts too."

"I do. I have seen them since I was about your age."

Aaron only nodded and led me into his bedroom.

"Are they here?"

"Yes."

I told Teresa that I would bless the house and asked if she wanted to follow me. She said that both her and Aaron would tag along, so I used a smudge stick that had white sage and lavender in it and began offering a protection prayer. I went into each room and then went outdoors—something I don't always do—but I was nudged to go that way. I stopped as we approached the south side of the house.

"What is here?"

"What do you mean?" Teresa asked me.

"Buried here. What is here?"

"Oh, there are unmarked graves here," she explained.

I rolled my eyes, relit the smudge stick, and began again.

Going back into the house, I told the family that I was done.

Aaron shook his head. "No, Kristy, they are still in my room."

"Show me," I asked.

Again, he took my hand and walked me to his room. "Right there."

Hidden in the corner was a spirit of a thin man. He told me that his name was Saul and that his farm was nearby. He looked to be in his 70s and his clothing was from the early 1900s. Although he didn't appear to be evil or negative, I could understand why Aaron wasn't sleeping.

Before I could offer the ghost's name, Aaron said, "I call him Saul."

I looked at Teresa in disbelief and asked to speak to her in private, so she put a DVD on for Aaron to watch while we talked.

I expressed my concerns over the burial site at the validation of the name. She said that there was a farm nearby who was owned by a man named Saul and it was believed that it was his family who was buried next to their home. She knew that Aaron had called his imaginary friend that, but hadn't put two and two together. It made sense to her now.

I went back into Aaron's room and had a chit-chat with Saul, informing him that he was causing problems to the little boy's sleep patterns and asked him to move on. He looked pitiful at me, as if he wasn't sure where to go. I asked him if he wanted help into the light and he nodded. He grabbed a small silver cat in spirit that I hadn't noticed before and allowed me to walk them into the light.

It is scary enough being an adult and seeing spirits or obtaining information from the Other Side, but when you are a child and you are inundated with things that others just cannot see, it is downright frightening. It can cause behavior problems, sleep problems, and misdiagnosis of everything from ADD to Autism, but there are some things that you can do that may be able to assist you in the situation. The first and foremost thing is to support your psychic child. The second is to take time to meditate and be quiet for just a few minutes with your child, as it will help them to regain themselves. It is also important to encourage them to journal, or if too young, journal the information that you receive from them.

When my daughter was three-years-old, we were sitting down playing a game when she started to recall a time when there was a fire. She asked me if I remembered the house fire and when her dad saved her brother and I. She later went on to say that she was very sad when I died from the smoke. Obviously, I was still alive and there had never been a fire. What she was recalling was a past life. In the end, she helped me grow because I had always been frightened of fire and never knew why. It was then that I embraced past lives. Growing up in the religious household that I had, it was something that only New Age kooks believed in. As soon as I embraced it, many puzzle pieces fell into place for not only my life, but for my own child's life. Why were they so bored with school? Well, because they already lived a lifetime and went through school. Sounds like agony to me too! Why could they recall historical moments in time that were undocumented, but very believable? Because they lived those times. Writing the information out is a truly powerful tool to go back to. Those things may also help explain fears.

I had one little girl that was petrified of a freezer. Absolutely petrified. When I 'read' her, the Spirit Guides explained that she had been locked in a stand-up freezer in another lifetime as punishment. Once her parents understood that, they sympathized instead of becoming angered by what they noted as a stupid fear. Children do not know how to filter their psychic gift; they are open. It is us adults—not just parents, but teachers, friends' parents, etc.—who help close that psychic door.

Aaron is sleeping much better and, although he is still a very sensitive little boy, his mom understands not to discredit everything that he says. Sometimes what seems like an overly imaginative child is actually something so much deeper.

# Ken

> "*A house is never still in darkness to those who listen intently;*
> *there is a whispering in distant chambers,*
> *an unearthly hand presses the snib of the window, the latch rises.*
> *Ghosts were created when the first man awoke in the night.*"
>
> — **J.M. Barrie**

My cell phone chirped and I answered on the first ring. "Hi Lisa!"

"I need you to come NOW!" my friend said in a panicked voice.

"What is wrong?" I asked. Lisa was one of my best friends and typically a calm spirit so it took me by surprise to hear the anxiety in her voice.

"Well, remember my sister's ghost?" Lisa asked.

"Yes," I answered, smiling at the experience I had with him almost six months ago.

It was a sunny summer evening when I was asked to come to Corrine's home. The family had been experiencing a lot of activity and I had met Lisa, her sister, and her sister's husband over at the house to see if I could contact the spirit in the home. It was an easy connection as the spirit of a young male named Ken who had died in a bicycle accident began communicating. He at first was quiet, but then began to communicate through the flame of a candle. With the flame acting as a pendulum, he would answer 'yes' and 'no' questions and direct the flame left and right for 'no' and up and down for 'yes.' Ken passed away sooner than he should have and, although he wasn't upset, he also didn't want to cross into the light and was instead quite comfortable staying with my friend's family. Noises in the attic, once thought to be an animal that had snuck in via the attic fan, were affirmed to be Ken.

"Corinne and Adam are gone on a cruise and my niece is staying over there. Only thing is Ken is creating a disturbance like no other."

Without asking anything further, I got into the car to meet her at the home.

When I pulled up into the driveway, I chuckled to see that Lisa, her niece, and another sister were standing around outside the door. All looked too frightened to go in. Now, ghosts can be scary, but Ken had never exhibited a frightening energy and as odd as it may sound, the family actually enjoyed Ken being around and relished in his playful antics.

It seemed that Ken was creating all sorts of electronic disturbances, from the phone ringing to setting the house alarm off. All of the activity was scaring the poor innocent teen who had taken on the job of caring for their pets while the couple went on a vacation.

Climbing up to the attic to have a chat with the deceased teen, the energy of the room felt heavy with sadness. I reassured him that he hadn't lost Corrine and Adam...that they were only on a trip and would be back. I again asked if he would think of crossing into the light where family members were most certainly going to greet him, but he only shook his head and stomped around the attic so much that Lisa called up to see if all was okay. It most certainly was...Ken was just having a tantrum.

The rest of the week was quiet and, when the couple returned, Ken gave them the silent treatment so much that they thought he may have left, but his stomping and his frightening the animals started back up a week later. Corrine would talk to Ken everyday and share her love for him, but also tell him that an attic was no place for him to live his eternal life and to instead cross. One day he finally gave in.

The home is quiet now, but everybody knows that Ken is in a much better place.

# 13

## Hoping to be Haunted

> "Houses are not haunted.
> We are haunted,
> and regardless of the architecture
> with which we surround ourselves,
> our ghosts stay with us until we ourselves are ghosts."
>
> — Dean Koontz

Denise was done. She was so ready to be out of the house and out of the marriage, but her lawyer told her that she had to hold tight at least another month. She wasn't quite sure that she would be able to make it.

Denise and Brad had only been married two years, but had dated for five years before that. Denise said that she didn't have any clue that Brad was bipolar until they moved in together.

"One minute he would be happy and the next he would be screaming about something so minuscule. I could hardly stand it," Denise confessed.

It wasn't until his violence began to come through that she knew she had to end the union. If she didn't do the dishes the way he liked, he would break every single one and walk away, only to return and kiss her on the head with an apology. Or the time that he was so angry that she had hung their wedding picture too high up on the wall — he grabbed the photo and hurled it across the hallway. She asked him to go to counseling, but he thought it was her that had the problem and that she needed to grow thicker skin. It became mind games that she couldn't stand.

Denise shared her story with me one warm summer evening. Inviting me to the marital home, we sat out on the back deck that overlooked the lake. "When Brad and I found this home, we were so excited," Denise said, tears streaming down her face. "I never imagined that I would be getting divorced."

The home was surrounded by many lakes and farmlands and was a 1980s construction colonial. It sat stately with its large white pillars and blood-red brick face on over two acres of land.

"I suppose what I really want to know is if the house has something in it or if it truly is Brad that has a problem. Maybe Brad is possessed by something," Denise hopefully said.

I felt as if I were put on the spot. More than ever I wanted to tell Denise that I could wave a magic wand and make all of her marital problems go away, but as I explored the four bedroom colonial, I found it peaceful, except for one area… the marital bedroom.

"We still sleep in the same bed," Denise whispered. "I suppose that I was hoping that perhaps he would change and become the Brad that I once knew. Leaving the bedroom would make it…" she briefly hesitated, "…real."

I didn't pick up on any apparition or feel spirit activity… only an anger that was felt in the fibers of the environment. Denise was upset and emotional over the divorce and Brad was angry and in denial over a mental illness. It was normal for any sensitive to pick up on what was happening.

"Well, have you had any unusual things happen?" I asked.

"Only one thing. Brad was downstairs. We had just gotten into a huge fight and I stormed up to the room. As I tried to come to grips with my emotions, I saw these three black shadows twirl around the room and fly out the window. I thought that perhaps I was imagining it, but Brad later said that he saw three large shadows staring at him around the same time that I had my encounter."

Denise looked at me hopeful, as if she had just handed me the last piece of the puzzle and I was supposed to share my conclusion.

"It only happened once?"

"Yes. Just once."

"Emotion can cause a portal of sorts for negative entities and perhaps that one argument opened up a doorway. I don't think that is the reason for Brad's mood changes. It certainly doesn't help things, especially if he is sensitive, but it isn't an explanation and I don't have a fix."

Denise looked fallen, but I had to be honest.

"I can bless the house and you can urge Brad again to see his physician," I offered.

I did my part, but Denise later told me that Brad was still suggesting that it was her and not him. A month later, their divorce was final and Denise moved out of the home. Recently she corresponded with me to tell me she was getting re-married and was extremely happy. She also shared that Brad still resided in the home and had not progressed in his life, but she had washed her hands of the past.

I can't say that a haunting is an easy explanation for negative things that happen in life; however, it can sometimes act as a piece of the unexplained puzzle. It wasn't this time around.

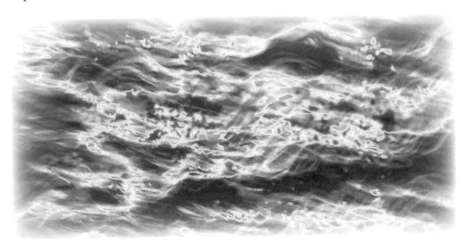

# 14

## Summoning the Spirits

R emember, early on in this book, I stated two things you should not do — DON'T conduct a séance and DON'T use an Ouiga Board. Well, these next two stories illustrate why.

### Office Ghost

The small professional building looks like every other office plaza, but this one is different. Not only did it house accountants, attorneys, and therapists, but it also employed one very active spirit. Wisps of smoke, smells of the dead, and doors opening and closing were just a few of the complaints that the tenants shared with me.

"One Saturday I came into the office to get some work done," Margaret, a pretty redhead, said. "There were no cars in the parking lot. For the most part, we can tell who is here even if we don't work in the same office. Well, I unlocked my office door and went to the restroom. The light was on, which I thought was strange since it's on a sensor. I peeked under the stalls, but I didn't anybody. Just as I pulled the latch on the closest stall, the far toilet flushed. I just stood there in fear. I admit that I didn't immediately think it was a ghost. My first thought was that someone had snuck into the building, but the

**This office building is haunted by a ghost that opens doors, flushes toilets, pounds on keyboards, and turns lights on and off.**

longer that I stood there and didn't hear any noises, I realized that *nobody* was there. Instead of using the facilities, I went back to my office and started working on some paperwork when my door opened. It just opened right up. I packed up my work and headed home as quickly as I could."

The employees said that it didn't matter whether it was day or night, a Monday or a Sunday...the spirit of the office made its presence known.

"Several of us decided to hold a séance to see if we could figure out who was haunting the building. Four of us sat around a small card table and asked for signs that it was here with us," Cody said.

"And boy did we get signs," Randi laughed. "The spirit started to rattle the ceiling and then we heard knocks and creaks. The most concrete evidence that we received, however, was when the card table began to rock back and forth in answer to our questions."

"We finally ended the séance," Margaret said. "We did it out of curiosity, but it became almost too much."

The rest of the gang nodded their heads in agreement.

After the séance, the activity continued.

"The worst was when I smelled spoiled food. I searched all over the office checking in desks, garbage cans, everywhere. Just as I was getting frustrated, the smell dissipated."

Footsteps, pacing up and down the hallway, doors opening and closing, and even papers floating in the air are other experiences the employees have encountered over several years.

One of the main complaints the tenants had was hearing the computer keyboards clicking as if someone was typing, but nobody being there. Several times gibberish would be found on the screen.

During my baseline investigation, I could feel a heaviness in the building and I sensed a spirit of a male.

You may ask how I know female from male spirits and the way that I sense it is that a female's energy feels lighter while a male's has a heavier feeling.

"Do you want me to rid the office of the ghost," I inquired.

"I would almost miss the ghost if it left," Margaret confessed. "If something is misplaced or out of place, he is an easy blame."

Some people just don't want to get rid of their spirits. This was the situation with this case. They just wanted to share their story.

# Haunted Hurons

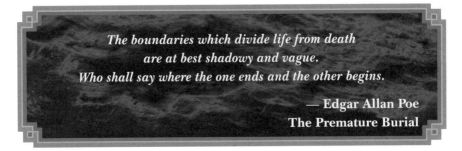

*The boundaries which divide life from death
are at best shadowy and vague.
Who shall say where the one ends and the other begins.*

— Edgar Allan Poe
**The Premature Burial**

I was asked to give readings to the incoming freshmen at Eastern Michigan University. "Offer them some hope and lessen their anxiety," I was told.

I could do that. My readings were never doom and gloom, and although I didn't filter out the good, bad, or ugly, I was still careful to keep my words positive and leave them feeling as if they had a plan of action and hope.

It was a warm August evening when I entered McKenny Hall. The kids were doing several different activities from eating food to purchasing school apparel to looking over their class schedules. I was just another form of entertainment. The hall stood in all its glory and I basked in its beauty as I made my way up the staircase where the committee had set me up. A line had already begun to form as I sat down at the table. I took in some deep breaths, centering myself. I was scheduled for three hours of readings with each student allowed ten minutes of my time. I had an ominous feeling that the three hours was going to feel like forever. The readings ran the gambit of those mourning their grandparents, to concern over choice of major, to several who had romantic problems or wanted to know if they would meet 'the one' soon.

All was fine until the end of the night. I was just about to pack up when a handsome young male, dressed in an Eastern Michigan University shirt, politely asked me for my time. He looked nervous, his eyes darting to a room down the hallway. I asked him what the problem was and he asked me to follow him. I gathered up my bags and he led me to a room just down the hall. In the middle of a table sat an Ouija board and six other students who all shared the same guilty look. The room felt thick and angry.

I took a seat and asked them what happened.

"We thought that we would try to summon Mary Fleszar, Jan Mixer, Alice Kalom, or Karen Beineman," the male told me, playing nervously with his shirt.

I groaned. Since I was young, I had been a reader of serial killers. I even had a run-in with Ted Bundy when I was just a child, so I was no stranger to the names that they listed. They were all victims of John Norman Collins — the Ypsilanti Killer — and all grotesquely murdered. They also all had ties to Eastern Michigan University.

"And," I asked, "what happened?"

The students just stared at me. I smirked at them and again asked for an explanation. A petite girl with long brown hair answered in a shaky voice.

"The board began to shake. We pulled our hands away, but the board still shook. So we stopped."

"An Ouija Board is nothing to mess with," I warned. "It is actually an open invitation for whatever to come through. You gave 'them' an open doorway to do whatever," I said swirling my hands up in the air.

I was most concerned because this was the beginning of the school year and the atmosphere of the environment was one of anticipation, frustration, and nerves. I was nervous because these spirits can act as parasites to individuals who have low self esteem, are having an identity crisis, or are going through a stressful time. Ding, ding, ding...sounds like any college freshman, right?

I told them that I would smudge them along with the Hall. I handed them my business card and urged them to call me *anytime* if they experienced anything that they felt was strange or uncomfortable, and I left them with one more warning.

"Do not try to communicate with them. They are not your friends! Do not convince yourself to feel comfortable with them around, even if they seem friendly, and most important, don't make deals with them. Call me instead."

"So you are like a Ghost Buster?" a male student asked.

I grinned and nodded. "You can call me that, if you like."

Every time I pass by McKenny Hall I shake my head and wrap it in white light. Kids will be kids, but for some an Ouija board is like handing a kid matches. It is nothing to play with.

# 15

# Ghost in the Woods

**M**adelyn contacted me via Internet complaining of activity in her family's home. Her bedroom was downstairs and she was feeling as if she was continually watched. She wanted it to stop. I immediately scheduled a visit out to her house the following weekend to investigate, but first asked if her parents were okay with me coming. Receiving assurance that they were anxious for me to assist, the next morning I packed up my car and made my way near Clarkston, Michigan. My husband looked for a reaction as we drove down the road, obviously feeling the energy.

"Yep, there is something here," I confirmed without him asking.

"Thought so too," he replied.

Chuck isn't psychic, but he is quite sensitive, whether he wants to admit it or not. He often tells clients that my so-called gift rubbed off on him and he didn't much like it.

We were immediately greeted in the driveway by the family's pups and allowed them to walk us to the door where I was met by Madelyn and her dad Roger. We sat at the dining room table for a bit and chatted. I asked them the usual questions — how they had been experiencing activity, how old the house was, and who was experiencing the haunting. They both explained that they all had felt a presence, but that the house was fairly new and so they weren't sure it was connected to the house. I wasn't so sure that they were right.

Taking a walk-through of the home, I was drawn to the furniture. It was an odd thing for me to be drawn too, but there were several mirrors and several pictures that I kept staring at. Madelyn's father noticed and told me that he traveled all over the world and always brought back a piece with him wherever he went. It was then that I realized that the psychometry piece of my gift was going into overdrive.

Psychometry is the ability to feel or sense the history of an inanimate object and of those who had owned, touched, or been around the object. With so many objects that didn't belong to the family per se, I was picking up on everybody who had ever owned the object and my senses were going off the charts to the point I was developing a headache. It was pretty similar to when I went into an antique or thrift store, which is why I don't.

To clear my head, I decided to go outside. As I was touring the home, I kept feeling this presence that was watching me. Madelyn decided to stay in, but Roger came with me. I began to put sea salt around the home in order to put a shield around their property, but when we got to the east side of the home, the woods next to us began to violently shake. We both looked at one another startled. There was no wind and we didn't have an animal that large here in Michigan to cause the amount of shaking. I threw sea salt in the woods, said a quick prayer, and the shaking immediately stopped. We nervously laughed and continued on our way, with a glance every so often back to the woods. We got to the front of the property when I felt an incredible sadness and inquired if he knew anything about the land. Roger nodded and told me that a car accident had occurred only a few years back and two teenagers were killed. It all made sense. I attempted to sense their presence and couldn't. I shared that with both Roger and

Madelyn when I returned to the home. That was a good thing, as it meant that they weren't grounded spirits. The energy could possibly have been imprinted as a residual haunting—a haunting that acted as a recording—but it still didn't explain the woods.

After doing another round inside the house, I offered some advice on how to cleanse the excess energy off their furniture and left asking them for updates. I was truly exhausted with the investigation due to the amount of energy and even fell asleep on the way home.

Roger continued to bring home his treasures, but he also made certain to smudge them before they came into the home..."just in case." Madelyn also said that although she still felt watched every once in awhile, it wasn't as frequent and she felt as if she could take care of it. She regained her room and her fears.

# 16

# Winged Creatures

*"From ghoulies and ghosties
And long-leggedy beasties
And things that go bump in the night,
Good Lord, deliver us!"*

— Scottish prayer

oseanna had been working long hours and sleeping less than five hours a night, but she couldn't help it. She was a single mom trying to take care of two little kids and was doing the best that she could. She hated her home in Warren, but again, she was doing the best that she could. She was frustrated.

One of the things that Roseanna was very good at — if you wanted to call it that — was astral travel. She could leave her body and travel to different locations. This was one of the reasons why she didn't feel that she was sleeping because, in essence, she wasn't. One November evening, she woke up looking over herself in astral travel mode. She explained that she was half in bed and half watching, but it was different than she had ever encountered. It was frightening.

"I hear this tapping on my bedroom window and feel petrified, but feel that I need to look anyway. I draw back the curtains and there is a winged demon staring at me. He was gray colored with pink hue wings. Every vein was sticking out of his body and his arms looked like that of a dinosaur as they curved. One claw had three long nails and the other had four. He tapped with just one finger on my window and smiled evil. He began to drool and for a brief moment I felt paralyzed. I finally threw my spirit into my body, jumped out of bed, and ran to the bathroom where I threw up. Figuring that it was just a nightmare, I went back to bed and once again heard tapping on the window and once again I pull back the curtains. I know that I sound incredibly stupid, but I felt this pull to look. He is still there, drooling and smiling, his eyes fire red and his claws becoming longer, retracting like a cat's would. He tells me mentally that he is roaming and there are more of him. My backyard turns into an army of these demons, but they aren't clones…they each have different features and colors. I woke up again and couldn't shake it."

It is extremely important that if you are prone to astral travel to protect yourself before you go to bed. Roseanna probably ended up in an ugly astral plane do to her exhaustion and lack of nurturing herself. She has since reported that she hasn't encountered anything so crazy, but that she makes it a ritual to say a quick prayer of protection before she goes to sleep and keeps several crystals on her bedside that she believes has an angelic vibration so that she doesn't 'wander' too far.

# 17

## An Unexpected Souvenir

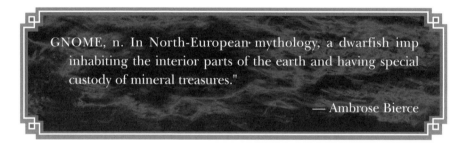

GNOME, n. In North-European· mythology, a dwarfish imp inhabiting the interior parts of the earth and having special custody of mineral treasures."

— Ambrose Bierce

O ne of my most interesting cases didn't involve ghosts at all, but something out of the fairy tale books. When the homeowner first contacted me, I thought perhaps she had been watching too many commercials where little gnomes with red hats traveled the world. But then she told me her story and I was entranced.

It was a Sunday evening in July when the family returned from their vacation to Myrtle Beach. Exhausted and sunburned, they returned back to their home in Michigan aching to be back by the ocean. One of the things that the kids loved about the sea was collecting shells. The family had carted bags and bags of different types of shells, along with much of the sand that came along with a beach trip.

Jill, a creature of habit, set her glasses down on the nightstand next to her bed and fell asleep. The trip took well over fourteen hours to get home and with four kids in the car, sleep was her reprieve from the real world. Jill woke up in the middle of the night and reached for her glasses, but they weren't there. Puzzled, she thought perhaps the cat had taken them; although unusual for him, she thought maybe he was angry about them taking a vacation without him. She got up, used the restroom, and saw that Sean, her husband, had fallen asleep on the couch and their cat Sylvester was sound asleep at his feet. She covered them both with a blanket and made her way to the bedroom, but as she reached her doorway, she was startled to see a small shadow running from her nightstand under her bed. She raced back into the living room and woke up a not to happy Sean.

"It's probably the cat," Sean mumbled.

"The cat is right there," Jill pointed.

"Mphhh," Sean answered, falling back to sleep.

Jill went back into the bathroom and put in her contacts since she was blind without her glasses. Heading back to the room, she again saw a shadow race across her room. Sure now that there was a mouse or a rat in there, she grabbed the afghan off of Sean and fell asleep on the love seat in the living room.

"What was that all about?" Sean asked in the morning over breakfast.

"What was what?" Jill replied, irked that he didn't come to her rescue.

Sean rolled his eyes, waiting for a response.

"My glasses disappeared and when I got up in the middle of the night, I saw something run across my room at full speed. I need you to look for me. Please," Jill pleaded.

Sean and Jill tore the room apart looking for her glasses. He moved the nightstand away from the wall and reached in a tiny hole in the back and pulled out her glasses.

"How?" Jill asked bewildered.

"Not a clue," Sean nonchalantly answered, walking away to brush his teeth.

A few days later, Jill was in the family room in the basement watching television when Sean came running downstairs.

"I saw something run underneath your dresser, on to the bed, and under it," he said breathlessly.

"What is it?" Jill squealed. She was a bit perplexed, as it took a lot for Sean to react.

"It was grey...the size of a child, but it had a beard," Sean replied. "It sort of looked like a gnome."

"A gnome?" Jill laughed. "Did you forget to take your medication?"

"Very funny," Sean answered dryly.

Sean moved every single piece of furniture only to find absolutely nothing. No rodent, no bug...*and no gnome*.

Another week passed and there weren't any gnome sightings...until the following weekend when the kids were watching television in Jill and Sean's bedroom. They came running out, screaming that something ran on top of the dresser and then under the bed. Sean raced to the room and once again tore it a part, finding absolutely nothing.

"We can't all be hallucinating. Can we?" Jill laughed.

The next morning at work, Jill was doing paperwork when her friend and coworker Michelle came by to chat. Jill felt silly, but felt as if she needed to share the gnome story, so she did.

Michelle laughed and explained, "You do have a gnome."

"What?" Jill said. "There are no such things as gnomes."

"Gnomes are considered imaginary creatures," Michelle explained, "but they are truly real. They are elementals and guardians of the earth. You probably brought one back from your trip."

Jill looked at Michelle as if she had lost her mind.

"You brought back shells, right?"

"Yessss..."

"That gnome is probably the keeper of the shells. You stole his shells and he probably wants them back."

"I can't drive back to Myrtle Beach," Jill said sarcastically. "Can't he just get over not having his shells?" Jill couldn't believe she was having this conversation.

"Put them in your garden and ask for his forgiveness. It should be okay after that." Michelle got up and went back to her office.

When Jill got home, she went looking for the shells and was surprised to find that they were still in the suitcase underneath her bed. Taking each and every bag of shells, she went out in the backyard and scattered them while talking to the 'imaginary' gnome. Asking for its forgiveness, she explained that they had just admired the shells so much. Since then, there have been no more gnome sightings.

# 18

# Living with Ghosts

## The Shadow Man

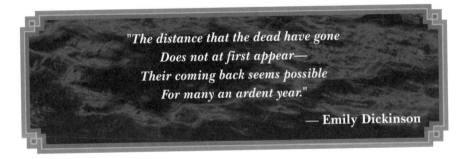

*"The distance that the dead have gone
Does not at first appear—
Their coming back seems possible
For many an ardent year."*

— Emily Dickinson

I knew that the house was haunted when I bought it and truthfully I was just fine with it. It never felt dark or ominous, but instead I felt as if someone was protecting me. Not to say that nothing ever creepy or crazy happened because it did, but that was just part of my life.

I had just moved into my new home and had just started dating my now husband, Chuck, when I asked him where the nearest fire station was. He looked at me with question, but drove by the building and pointed it out. I nodded, unaware of why I asked. Two weeks after moving in, the kids were at their dad's home and I was left only with Guinness, my

Australian Shepherd. After working all day, I ate a quick bite to eat and decided to do some laundry. I put a load of wash in the washer and placed the wash I had done before I left for work into the dryer. My eyes felt heavy, so I thought that since it was only 7 p.m., I would just lay down real quick and get up to switch the wash. Instead, I ended up falling asleep. I woke up to hearing what sounded like an alarm clock, with high pitched chimes ringing. It sounded like it was next to my ear. Startled, I looked at the clock and it was after 3 a.m. I sat up in bed and had a horrible feeling. The house smelled of natural gas and Guinness was looking lethargic. The ringing continued, but I couldn't place it. It wasn't the carbon monoxide detector or the smoke alarm, but it was loud and moved with me. I ran downstairs to the basement to find that my dryer was still going and it smelled like a fire, so I ran back upstairs, grabbed Guinness and my cell phone, and dialed 911. It was just a few minutes before the firemen arrived. A small fire had started in my dryer's lint trap and the home was filled with gas. They put out the fire and opened up all of the windows and told me to sleep somewhere else. I asked them about the high-pitched alarm and the fireman's eyebrows furled in question. He said that no alarms were going off and that I was very lucky that I woke up when I did.

The feeling of a presence continued to be felt even after the fire incident. It never upset Guinness or the kids, but it did many friends and relatives that came to visit. Sitting in my living room, it would feel as if a shadow would hover over you. I had more than one friend cut their visit short because of the ominous presence. I always laughed it off that they were being sissies because what I referred to as the Shadow Man was completely innocent.

Although the kids weren't troubled by his presence, he would often wake them up and they both started to leave the light on in their rooms..."just on the safe side."

My line of work made my home a haven for spirits. Chuck actually came to me on more than one occasion and told me that the home was getting too crowded and I needed to do something. If any normal person had witnessed the conversation, they would have thought it insane. How overcrowded was a home with two kids, him, and I? But you have to take into account the furniture being moved when we would come home from work, the clocks that would just stop working, the noises, the door slamming, and the dark shadows that would creep along the hallway.

It was summertime when we adopted Oswald, a friendly black cat. Ozzy and Guinness adored one another and we thought that it would all be just fine. The only thing was that we didn't check in with the house spirit. Either the Shadow Man disliked Ozzy or Ozzy just plain didn't like the Shadow Man, as Ozzy would run up and down the hallway, climbing the walls the whole way. He would howl and walk away, hair puffed out in fright. It took several months before they came to an agreement to just ignore one another. Ozzy stayed out of the hallway and the Shadow Man didn't invade Ozzy's basement. Life at the Robinett home was once again quiet.

## Fox & Hounds

When my husband and I were looking for a place to hold our wedding reception, we were obviously looking for good food and a nice atmosphere and came upon Fox & Hounds in Bloomfield Hills. The haunted part was a bonus.

A month or so before our wedding, we went to Fox & Hounds to solidify our reception plans and order our wedding cake. The restaurant, which was used previously as an old English style inn, was founded in 1928 and boasted an elaborate clientele. Entering the large wooden doors and turret that were reminiscent of a castle, you were taken back in time. Catering to the wealthy, you could almost see the ghosts of past patrons hidden in the fibers of time.

Because of my profession, I am always looking for a good ghost story and so I went in search of staff with tales and there was no lack of them at the restaurant. One waitress told me that several times a week the pots and pans would crash down off their shelves. The cooks would pick them up, only to turn around and have them on the floor once more. They also often heard conversations with both females and males, but nobody would be there and no voices carried from the street. There were two rooms in which they felt a presence and that was the basement at the bar and a small banquet room with a fireplace that sat away from the dining room, next to the stairway of the basement. Other employees told me that they would smell a pipe in the banquet room and yet nobody would be in the building. Yet another employee explained that one time when she was going down the stairway, she felt someone inappropriately grope her. She twirled around, but nobody was there.

Our wedding day, October 14, 2006, started off a tad bit dramatic with soon-to-be stepdaughter, Molly, spraining her ankle and having to go to the hospital mere hours before the service. While Chuck took off for the hospital, Cooper, our Siberian Husky, inhaled a months' worth of blood pressure medication (and lived). So either my ghost antenna wasn't up that night or the spirits had taken the night off. Neither myself nor my party had any experiences, but I did in June 2007.

I decided to hold a paranormal conference at the location and met with the manager of the Fox & Hounds. The restaurant was not open to the public and so I was able to wander and get a feel for the place. As I went back into the room where our wedding reception was held, I was surprised to see the spirit of an older gentleman sitting in the chair next to the fireplace. He sat there, ice blue eyes, looking at me as if to ask why I was disturbing him.

The manager asked me to sit down at the table and, while he continued to go over the paperwork, I couldn't help but sense the spirit. My agitation must have shown because the manager asked me if I was okay. I explained what I was seeing. He looked at me surprised and said that the same man had been seen several times and asked me to describe him in detail. It wasn't hard to do — the man looked like flesh and blood to me, but I was the only one who could see him. Heavy set, he wore a navy blue suit and looked as if he belonged to the restaurant. He was very comfortable sitting next to the fireplace and kept pointing to a picture above that displayed hunting dogs. He never once smiled, only stared at me. After giving the description, he dissipated.

I excused myself and went to the Ladies Room. I tried to open the stall door, only for it to feel stuck. I tried again — again, it felt stuck — so I went to the next one. Once more it wouldn't budge. It was as if it was painted shut. I shrugged and tried the first one again and it swung out easily. I am not sure if I was more excited or stunned at the activity just because I hadn't had any the previous year when I was there. After settling back down at the table to discuss the event, the manager asked if I wanted a tour. He showed me and my husband around and told us about the legend of the basement. Apparently there had been a tunnel that ran underneath the restaurant, across the road during prohibition. Thought to be a part of the Purple Gang, who were Jewish Gangsters, the Inn was kept flowing with liquor to make the elite happy. Although there were no findings of a tunnel, it was thought that this illegal behavior from the notorious gang, which had connections to Al Capone, had possibly left remnants of different types of spirits locked in the tunnels.

It was unfortunate that a few months before our conference was to be held, I received a phone call from the manager explaining that the restaurant had been sold and would be torn down. This beautiful historical landmark was indeed destroyed in 2008, forever trapping many of its haunting secrets.

# 19

## Blanche

The town of Plymouth, Michigan is well blended with turn-of-the-century Victorian homes that date back to the late 1800s to more contemporary style houses and condominiums. There is always something to do in this charming town, whether it's getting ice cream, enjoying the band play at the pavilion, or perhaps perusing an art and crafts display at Kellogg Park. Near Kellogg Park, which sits in the center of town, is a gorgeous home that lends

The Wilcox House

This is the site of a Plymouth Landmark, the Wilcox House, built in 1903 by William Markham, inventor of the BB Gun and the co-founder of the Daisy Air Rifle Co. George and Harriet Wilcox purchased it in 1911 and here raised their three children, Julia, Katherine, and Johnston ("Jack").

Originally, in the side yard, a continuously flowing fountain spilled over into a large reflection pool. A pergola, gazebo and statuary were focal points on the extensively landscaped grounds. The grounds also proudly displayed exotic plants, unusual trees and rare shrubs that Mr. Markham imported from around the world, including Amabilis Peonies, and Ginkgo, Black Magnolia and Copper Beech trees. During World War II, as part of the war effort, the home was converted into five apartments.

Fulfilling a bequest of Jack Wilcox, who was born in the house and lived there for most of his 83 years, the stunning 10 foot stained glass window, that was originally in the Solarium on the first floor, was donated to the Plymouth Historical Museum where it now creates a dramatic entryway display.

Just before he died in June, 2000, Jack Wilcox sold the property with the vision that an attractive condominium project would be built around the house and with the hope that the house would be preserved so that it might continue to shine as a symbol of the City of Plymouth and serve as a vivid reminder of its storied past.

itself too much history, but also many secrets... and, according to some, spirits.

The inventor of the BB Gun and co-founder of the Daisy Air Rifle, William Markham built a grand Queen Anne Victorian and named it Markham Park. With gardens, statues, and fountains, the home was quite well known for miles around. Although admired for its architectural elegance, those who resided in Plymouth were not at all thrilled with the story behind the house.

William built the home for his secretary and mistress Blanche Shortman. William, himself, lived with his family not far from the grandiose home. The town, being religious and conservative, snubbed their noses at what they thought was over-the-top arrogance. However, William, who had asked his wife for a divorce several times and was turned down each and every time, felt that this was his only way of keeping the lady that he loved.

Once William's wife passed away, he moved in with Blanche, but the gossip from the other residents was too much. They sold the home and moved to California.

The talk didn't stop, however, even after the Wilcoxs purchased the home. Even today, over one hundred years later, there is talk of spirits. Eyewitnesses have claimed to see a lady dressed in white depart from the now abandoned home. They say that she exits the wrought iron gates and makes her way to the park, where she sits and stares, as if waiting for her true love, William, to meet her. Many

**The Wilcox House, originally known as Markham Park, is currently being restored to her original glory.**

believe this is a case of a residual haunting in lieu of an intelligent one.

A man in his early 70s explained to me that it was October and dusk was setting in when he was walking his dog. He saw a lady dressed in a long white gown come from the Wilcox home, cross the street, and make her way to the park. He stopped and asked her if she needed help. He said hat he knew that nobody lived in the home and was confused as to why someone would have been in it. The lady didn't respond...she just stood there. He didn't think anything of it until he saw a news article that the home was in need of restoration. Others in the town have similar claims, none thinking anything peculiar until later. They say that she looks like flesh and blood.

So perhaps, as you enjoy an evening in Kellogg Park, you too might catch a sight of the spirit many claim to be Blanche.

# 20

## Eloise

loise is one of the most talked about presumed haunted locations in the State of Michigan. Eloise was named after the Postmaster's four-year-old daughter who was intricate for getting the County House approved in 1894 when it became the sick, elderly, and insane. Known as the 'Crazy House,' Eloise actually began as a poor house, but evolved into a mental hospital in 1841 when it admitted its first insane patient.

**It is said that many past patients roam the halls of Eloise.**

"No Trespassing" signs are posted everywhere throughout the remnants of Eloise, as it is frequented by ghost hunters.

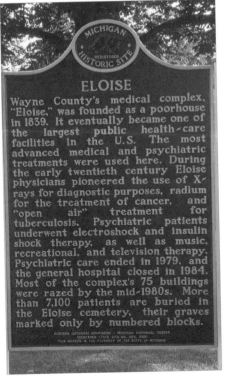

MICHIGAN
REGISTERED
HISTORIC SITE

ELOISE

Wayne County's medical complex, "Eloise," was founded as a poorhouse in 1839. It eventually became one of the largest public health-care facilities in the U.S. The most advanced medical and psychiatric treatments were used here. During the early twentieth century Eloise physicians pioneered the use of X-rays for diagnostic purposes, radium for the treatment of cancer, and "open air" treatment for tuberculosis. Psychiatric patients underwent electroshock and insulin shock therapy, as well as music, recreational, and television therapy. Psychiatric care ended in 1979, and the general hospital closed in 1984. Most of the complex's 75 buildings were razed by the mid-1980s. More than 7,100 patients are buried in the Eloise cemetery, their graves marked only by numbered blocks.

MICHIGAN HISTORICAL COMMISSION · MICHIGAN HISTORICAL CENTER
REGISTERED STATE SITE NO. 805, 2000
THIS MARKER IS THE PROPERTY OF THE STATE OF MICHIGAN

Eloise was a city within itself and housed everything from a dairy farm, a pig farm, greenhouses, a fire department, power plants, bakeries, a library, a post office, shops, and even a morgue and cemetery.

I interviewed a lovely lady who was in her 80s, who also happened to be named Eloise. She grew up just a few blocks from where Eloise stood and shared with me what it was like growing up near the institution.

"It was always creepy to go to Eloise. Often times I would see the patients swinging outside or just walking around the grounds. Once in awhile we would go there to mail packages at the post office and I hated it. The hospital had this dark feeling."

She further explained that the Eloise loomed over the city of Westland, which at that time was called Nankin Mills.

"It was rumored that the mentally ill and the poor were kept together for quite awhile until authorities found out and made them separate to different floors. Apparently they moved the poor where the farm animals had been housed and used inhumane restraints," Eloise continued. "There were times when I would be playing in my yard and I could swear I would hear screaming, but the adults would discount it as the farm animals. But I knew...I knew that the animals didn't make those noises. It was definitely human beings being tortured. It was later realized that most of those who were diagnosed as being insane actually had epilepsy or were bipolar."

Due to lack of funding, Eloise no longer exists and many of the buildings have been torn down with just a few still standing; however, each still hold the secrets that have long been kept within these walls.

Every year, many people attempt to sneak into the remaining facilities and land surrounding it. You will be arrested, as there are 'No Trespassing' signs posted everywhere. Not only is it illegal, it is dangerous. The remaining buildings are in ruins and are crumbling.

**One of the buildings still remain and acts as a County Office. Inside, you will find a museum dedicated to the history of Eloise.**

Said to have over eleven tunnels below the grounds, they were used to get to building to building without having to go out in the harsh Michigan winters. One such tunnel was also used to move the dead from the morgue to the nearby cemetery where they weren't even given tombstones, but a cement number.

Several businesses and even newer homes now sit on the remaining land. The employees shared that they had several ghostly experiences and felt that it had to do with the land that they stepped on.

"I wouldn't go there," Eloise whispered, shaking her head. "I just wouldn't want to run into any of those poor souls. They had a horrible life and now a horrible afterlife."

Video was taken on the grounds of Eloise. When played back, screams from what sounded like a little girl were loud and clear. It was enough to send chills down all who heard it.

# Appendix

*The following gives readers an idea as to the kind of confidentiality agreement clients should be offered at the time of an investigation.*

## Client Confidentiality Agreement

A very important aspect ghost hunting is privacy of the property owner. A haunting is a very sensitive topic and you should treat it so when completing an investigation. Most people do not want others to know of the situation, and so it is crucial to offer the client a Confidentiality Agreement that offers them the peace of mind that you won't be blabbering their situation to every Tom, Dick, and Harriet.

During the questionnaire period of an investigation, the property owners tend to divulge private information about their home, their family, and themselves, so it is imperative that you offer them a commitment.

Never discuss personal information with anyone outside of the organization. This applies to identity of the homeowner and location of the property.

Identify with certain character keys — in the report that you send back to the owner and/or post on your website — the resident while withholding names and initials.

Never sell or trade information with other investigators unless the property owner's authorize it. And although, research is often shared with others in the community, it has to be acknowledged that that data distributed never jeopardizes the identity or location.

# Homeowner Questionnaire

Whether you are a homeowner experiencing paranormal activity or you are a paranormal investigator aiding in an investigation, it is important to ask questions in order to get a better handle on the haunting, the cause of the haunting, or if there is, in fact, a haunting at all and the situation can be debunked. A typical questionnaire would include the following:

🌸 When did the activity first occur?

🌸 Who was the first person to discover the activity?

🌸 Who has experienced the activity?

🌸 Are their unusual smells?

🌸 Are their unusual noises?

🌸 What rooms or areas do the occurrences happen in?

🌸 Is there recent stress in the home?

🌸 Does anybody drink?

🌸 Does anybody do illegal drugs?

🌸 Is there anybody ill in the home?

🌸 Are their children in the home?

Some of these questions seem quite personal, however they help with the investigation. Even if there is an alcoholic in the home, that doesn't discount paranormal activity, but it may help explain who the spirit is feeding off of and why.

# Property Access Permission

It also is a good idea to offer the property owner a Property Access Permission form, or Disclaimer, which would grant the investigators access to the property and also release the owner of the location from any injuries that may occur during the course of the investigation. In addition, it should offer a clause that would hold the investigators harmless in case there were damages to the property.

It is very uncommon for anything to happen to the property or the person, but it is always best to be safe. And it is always best to check with an attorney if you have any questions.

## Social Contract

Many paranormal teams also create Social Contracts, or Mission Statements. Image is important in order to earn respect. One of the most important parts of investigating is that it is free-of-charge. There are other ways to earn money through the paranormal, but investigating should not be one.

Team T-shirts do not create an instant respect, but speaking, writing, and acting professional will spill over to others in the community more than matching shirts.

## Smudging Instructions

### The Environment

Smudging is a Native American ritual that is a simple and powerful way to remove negative energy.

Place several leaves of white sage (you can also use other types of herbs, such as sweet grass and lavender; however, I love how the sage works!) in a fireproof container or shell and light them. The flame will go out in a short time (if not, gently blow it out) and the sage will begin to smolder. Fan the smoke with your hand or with a feather. While walking around, speak out loud a blessing, protection, or a prayer — whatever you feel comfortable saying.

Begin the ritual by going to the farthest part of your house and working yourself towards the front, opening a window or door where you can draw all of the negative energy out. Every area should be 'cleaned,' including closets, basements, nooks and crannies, kitchen cabinets, and every other crevice that negative grime could hide.

You can use any prayer or mantra that feels appropriate for you and your beliefs. An example is:

"I ask God, the Archangels and my Guides to be with me. I ask that the White Light of the Holy Spirit surround and protect me and those in this home. I ask that you please cleanse and purify our souls. Release any negativity within the soul and within the home. I ask that the dark smoke be absorbed by the White Light, causing no harm. Please bless this house and all that are in it. Let nothing but love and positive energy pass through."

Often times Smudging needs to be done several times when experiencing a haunting and it may at first actually disturb the spirit. Think of it as an unwanted houseguest that you are trying to evict.

## Smudging Yourself

Many times it isn't the environment that is haunted — it is the person. By Smudging oneself, it helps keep the oppression of spirit activity away.

You can either do this yourself or have another person help you with it. Place several leaves of white sage in a fireproof container or shell and light them. The flame will go out in a short time (if not, gently blow it out) and the sage will begin to smolder. Fan the smoke with your hand or with a feather, beginning with your feet up to your head. Fan the smoke around you as you imagine it passing through you. Visualize the smoke drawing out all of the imperfections and negativity that have collected within and say a prayer of protection.

Be cautious with flame and/or heat from sage.

# Bibliography

Association of Graveyard Rabbits. *About the Association of Graveyard Rabbits (AGR)*, 2008. Accessed March 7, 2009 at http://about-gyra.blogspot.com

Clark, Alvin C. *A History of the Wayne County Infirmary, Psychiatric, and General Hospital Complex at Eloise, Michigan, 1832-1982.* Wyandotte, Michigan: Wyandotte Rotary Club, n.p. 1982.

DeWindt, Edwina. *Our Fame & Fortune in Wyandotte.* Wyandotte, Michigan: Wyandotte Rotary Club, 1985.

Freeman, Carol Willits. *Of Dixboro: Lest We Forget.* Dexter, Michigan: Freeman, 1979.

Kavieff, Paul R. *The Purple Gang: Organized Crime in Detroit 1910-1945.* Fort Lee, New Jersey: Barricade Books, 2000.

Keister, Douglas. *Stories in Stone: A Field Guide to Cemetery Symbolism and Iconography.* New York, New York: MJF, 2004.

Kerstens, Elizabeth Kelley. *Plymouth's First Century: Innovators and Industry.* Mount Pleasant, South Carolina: Arcadia Publishing, 2001.

Keyes, Edward. *The Michigan Murders.* New York, New York: Pocket Books, 1976.

# Index